FABULOUS FREEZER MEALS

FABULOUS FREEZER MEALS

over 200 great-tasting recipes to save time and money

Jenny Ahlstrom Stanger

Walnut Springs Press, LLC

110 South 800 West

Brigham City, Utah 84302

http://walnutspringspress.blogspot.com

ISBN:978-1-935217-38-1

To my husband, Mark, who has given me wings to fly. To my darling girls, Lyndi, Ashley, Ava, and Sierra, who fill my life with sunshine and joy. And to my mom and dad, who have always been there to cheer me on.

Contents

Author's Note

Fabulous Freezer Meals is a collection of recipes for great-tasting dishes that freeze well and that your family will love. This book will change the way you cook!

When I first started making freezer meals, I tried the "cook for one day, eat for one month" method, but it was way too complicated for me. In fact, it took me two weeks to finish the work that was supposed to take just one day! So, I came up with my own plan, and I'd like to share it with you.

Basically, this book teaches you how to stock your freezer with the basics, then make a few recipes every two weeks. (That only takes about two hours.) Your freezer will fill quickly with a variety of meals, and you will save time and money. Deciding what to have for dinner—and preparing it—will be stress free.

Check out my website, freezerdinner.com, for more great recipes. If you have any questions, feel free to contact me at freezerdinner@gmail.com. Best of luck!

Getting Started

Freezer Recipe Basics

Why Freezer Meals?

- Freezer meals save both time and money because you shop less, eat out less, and waste less food. How much money can you save? Depending on the size of your family, you could save up to $300 per month!
- Freezer meals are healthier than fast food and pre-packaged frozen foods.
- With freezer meals, you can cater to your family's tastes, and you can determine the portion sizes yourself.
- Freezer meals are convenient to take to friends who are ill or unable to cook for their family.
- Freezer meals can save you stress and last-minute trips to the grocery store when you need to prepare a meal for company.
- Freezer meals help ensure that your family eats at least one meal together each day, which can help strengthen family relationships.

How Long Do Frozen Foods Last?

Breads and breakfasts	2 months
Drinks and popsicles	2 months
Ice cream cakes	2 months
Main dishes	4 months
Salads, sides, and soups	4 months
Toffee and freezer jam	12 months

What Freezes Well?

- Cooked rice
- Bread dough
- Piecrusts
- Cookie dough
- Cinnamon rolls

- Muffins
- Burritos
- Waffles
- Shredded cheese
- Fajita mix

- Soups
- Pasta sauces
- Cooked ground beef
- Tofu
- Fish

- Grapes
- Broccoli
- Nuts
- Citrus peels
- Herbs

What Doesn't Freeze Well?

- Celery
- Eggplant
- Peaches

- Nectarines
- Plums
- Cream cheese

- Block cheese
- Mayonnaise
- Custards

- Frostings
- Raw meats*
- Cooked pasta

*Refreezing raw meats can cause them to lose moisture and become tough, but when marinated or mixed in a sauce, meats have more flavor and are usually more tender.

What Doesn't Freeze Well?

- Vegetables and fruits with a high water content (like celery, eggplant, and peaches) become soggy when frozen raw and defrosted. However, if you want to freeze them there are a few things you can do to help maintain their integrity. Frozen fruits are excellent when used in cobblers or smoothies. See "Stock Your Freezer: Bulk Recipes" on page 23 for tips on freezing vegetables.
- If frozen and thawed, cream cheese will dry out and crumble unless it is mixed with other ingredients. Block cheese also crumbles after thawing, so shred cheese before freezing it.
- Mayonnaise, custards (pumpkin pie included), and frostings do not freeze well, because they separate when thawed.
- Fully cooked noodles and fried foods will be soggy when defrosted. To solve this problem, only cook them 60% of the way, then cool and freeze. Bake frozen fried foods to finish cooking them.

Packaging

Usually, I use zip-top plastic bags to store food in the freezer. Any brand works fine, but make sure you double-bag soups and sauces. To prevent freezer burn, squeeze as much air out of the bag as possible before closing it completely. Lay bags flat in the freezer so that you can stack them like bricks. Defrost on high in a microwave-safe bowl in the microwave.

Because foods can change color in the freezer, **don't forget** to label packages with the cooking time and temperature, using a permanent marker. Example: "Lasagna, 350°F, 60 minutes."

I use disposable foil pans for lasagnas and other layered entrees. They are reusable and can be washed in the dishwasher. At a party or restaurant supply store, these pans cost as little as 40¢ each.

For one-dish entrees such as lasagna, use plastic wrap to line your pans before placing food in them. First line the dish, then place the food on top and freeze for 1 hour (flash freeze). Take the food and plastic wrap out of the dish and wrap the frozen meal in more layers of plastic wrap, then label and freeze. To serve, remove plastic and place frozen meal back in glass dish to defrost and cook.

Organize Your Freezer

Often, I hear people say, "I'll make freezer meals when I buy a big deep freezer." But investing in a deep freezer is only worthwhile if you can use all the food inside before it gets too old. I have a side-by-side refrigerator in my house and a small freezer/fridge combo in the garage. This works great for my family.

To keep organized, you will want to buy some stackable wire baskets for your refrigerator, or deep plastic baskets for a larger freezer. They need to be easy to pull out of the freezer so you don't have to keep the door open too long. Label the front of the baskets ("meats," "vegetables," "fruit," "rice and pasta," etc.) with self-laminating luggage tags or even paper zipped inside small plastic bags.

Kitchen Supplies Needed

Several permanent markers
2 extra-large plastic bowls for bulk mixing
2 sets of measuring cups (a set for dry ingredients and a set for wet ingredients)
1 large stockpot
2 sharp knives (a chef's knife and a serrated knife)
4 bread pans (metal)
Several boxes of zip-top gallon- quart-, and sandwich-size plastic bags (any brand)
Large box of plastic wrap (I buy an 18-inch x 3000-foot box of polyvinyl film [plastic wrap] from a membership warehouse)

Helpful Hint
To save yourself time, have your local butcher slice your beef roast into fajita strips, cube your ham, butterfly your chicken breasts, etc. They do these services free of charge at most grocery stores. (It's always nice to leave a tip.)

Safe Defrosting and Refreezing

Defrosting in the Refrigerator:

Most foods takes 24 hours to defrost in the refrigerator. Once food has defrosted in the refrigerator, even if it is uncooked, it is safe to refreeze it. However, there may be a decrease in quality because of the moisture lost in defrosting. Also, I often pour off some extra water when defrosting soups and salads.

Defrosting in the Microwave:

Use food right away if you have defrosted it in the microwave, because bacteria starts to multiply when food is warm.

It is safe to refreeze leftovers once food has been fully cooked. In addition, I often use individual meal-size plastic containers for quick frozen work lunches. Simply remove the plastic container and thaw the food in the microwave until hot, then enjoy.

Discard any leftovers that have been out of the refrigerator longer than three hours. Use refrigerated leftovers within four days. Harmful bacteria can multiply between 40 and 140°F.

Final Tip

Always wear comfortable shoes while you prepare, freeze, or cook food. Cooking barefoot in the kitchen can really take a toll on your body.

Standard Measurements

c = cup
fl = fluid
gal = gallon
lb = pound
liq = liquid
min = minute
mod = moderate

oz = ounce
pkg = package
pt = pint
qt = quart
t = tsp = teaspoon
T = Tbsp = tablespoon

Equivalency Chart

pinch or dash	=	less than ⅛ teaspoon
3 teaspoons	=	1 tablespoon
2 tablespoons	=	1 fluid ounce
4 tablespoons	=	¼ cup = 2 ounces
6 tablespoons	=	¾ cup
5⅛ tablespoons	=	⅓ cup
8 tablespoons	=	½ cup
16 tablespoons	=	1 cup
1 cup	=	8 fluid ounces
2 cups	=	1 pint
2 pints	=	1 quart
4 cups	=	1 quart
4 quarts	=	1 gallon
8 ounces (liquid)	=	1 cup
16 ounces (dry)	=	1 pound

Emergency Substitutions

- Active dry yeast (1 package): 2½ teaspoons dry yeast
- Allspice (1 teaspoon ground): ½ teaspoon ground cinnamon plus ½ teaspoon ground cloves
- Baking powder (1 teaspoon): ¼ teaspoon baking soda plus ½ teaspoon cream of tartar
- Baking soda (1 teaspoon): 1½ teaspoons baking powder
- Baking mix, 2 cups (if you're out of Bisquick): Mix 1¾ cups all-purpose flour, 2½ teaspoons baking powder, and ¾ teaspoon salt. Cut in ⅓ cup shortening until mixture looks like fine crumbs.
- Balsamic vinegar (1 tablespoon): 1 tablespoon sherry or cider vinegar
- Breadcrumbs, dry (¼ cup): ¼ cup finely crushed cracker crumbs, cornflakes, or quick-cooking or old-fashioned oats
- Brown sugar (1 cup firmly packed): 1½ tablespoons molasses (or corn syrup) plus 1 cup granulated sugar
- Buttermilk (1 cup): 1 tablespoon vinegar or lemon juice plus enough milk to make 1 cup. Let mixture stand for 5 minutes before using.
- Chili sauce (1 cup): 1 cup tomato sauce, ⅛ cup brown sugar, 2 tablespoons vinegar (white or apple), ¼ teaspoon cinnamon, dash of allspice, and dash of fresh ground cloves
- Cornstarch (1 tablespoon): 2 tablespoons flour
- Cream of tartar (1 teaspoon): 3 teaspoons lemon juice OR 3 teaspoons vinegar
- Fresh herbs (1 tablespoon): 1 teaspoon dried herbs
- Fish sauce (1 teaspoon): 1 teaspoon Worcestershire sauce or light soy sauce with salt
- Garlic (1 clove): ⅛ teaspoon garlic powder or minced dried garlic
- Half-and-half (1 cup): ⅞ cup milk plus 3 tablespoons butter
- Honey (1 cup): 1¼ cups sugar plus ¼ cup water or fruit juice
- Italian dressing packet mix (1 package): 1 tablespoon parsley, 2 teaspoons salt, 2 teaspoons sugar, 1 teaspoon garlic (bottled minced, or fresh), 1 teaspoon onion powder, ½ teaspoon basil, and ¼ teaspoon red pepper flakes

- Lemon, 1 medium (fresh juice): 2 to 3 tablespoons bottled lemon juice
- Lemon peel (zest), 1 teaspoon: ½ teaspoon lemon extract
- Marinade from scratch (per pound of meat; can be used with any meat): 4 tablespoons soy sauce, 1 tablespoon rice wine vinegar, 1½ teaspoons baking soda, and 1 tablespoon cornstarch
- Mustard, dry (1 teaspoon): 1 tablespoon prepared mustard
- Molasses (1 cup): 1 cup honey
- Onion (1 small): 1 teaspoon onion powder or 1 tablespoon minced dried onion
- Onion soup mix (one package): ¼ cup dried minced onion, 2 tablespoons instant beef bouillon, and ½ teaspoon onion powder
- Orange, 1 medium (fresh juice): ¼ to ⅓ cup store-bought orange juice
- Pumpkin pie spice (1 teaspoon): ½ teaspoon ground cinnamon, ¼ teaspoon ground ginger, ⅛ teaspoon ground allspice, and ⅛ teaspoon ground nutmeg
- Powdered sugar (1 cup): 1 cup sugar and 1 tablespoon cornstarch, mixed well in food processor
- Rice wine vinegar: rice vinegar or apple cider vinegar
- Self-rising flour (1 cup): 1 cup flour plus 1½ teaspoons baking powder plus ½ teaspoon salt
- Semisweet chocolate (1 ounce): 1 ounce unsweetened chocolate plus 1 tablespoon sugar
- Shortening (1 cup): 1 cup softened butter OR 1 cup margarine, omitting ½ teaspoon salt from recipe
- Sour cream (1 cup): ½ cup plain yogurt and ½ cup mayonnaise, OR 1 cup cottage cheese, puréed
- Sweetened condensed milk (1 can): Mix 2 cups instant dry powdered milk and ½ cup hot water in a blender, then add 1 cup sugar and 2 tablespoons butter. Combine well.
- Unsweetened chocolate (1 ounce): 3 tablespoons unsweetened cocoa plus 1 tablespoon margarine
- Tapioca (1 tablespoon): 1½ tablespoons flour
- Tomato sauce (2 cups): ¾ cup tomato paste plus 1 cup water
- Tomato juice (1 cup): ½ cup tomato sauce plus ½ cup water
- Vanilla bean (1 inch): 1 teaspoon vanilla extract
- Whole milk (1 cup): ½ cup evaporated milk plus ½ cup water
- Worcestershire sauce: bottled steak sauce
- Yogurt (plain, 1 cup): 1 cup sour cream or buttermilk

Alcohol Substitutions

Except where indicated, substitute equal amounts.

- Amaretto (2 tablespoons): ¼ to ½ teaspoon almond extract
- Beer: chicken broth, beef broth, or white grape juice
- Rum (light or dark): water, white grape juice, pineapple juice, apple juice, or apple cider
- Sake: rice vinegar
- Sherry or bourbon: orange or pineapple juice, peach syrup, or nonalcoholic vanilla extract
- Vermouth, dry: white grape juice, white wine vinegar, or nonalcoholic white wine
- Vermouth, sweet: apple juice, grape juice, balsamic vinegar, nonalcoholic sweet wine, or water with lemon juice
- White wine: water, chicken broth, white grape juice, or ginger ale
- Red wine: cranberry juice, chicken broth, beef broth, or flavored vinegar

Stock Your Freezer: Bulk Recipes

Meats

Bacon and Sausage

Yield: 2 pounds cooked bacon and sausage

Cook 2 pounds of sausage links and bacon on a broiler pan in the oven. Broil the meat until bacon is dark and sausage is browned. The grease will collect in the pan, and when the bacon is properly browned it is easy to crumble. Cool the meat and place in zip-top plastic bags to freeze.

To serve

Pull out frozen sausage or bacon as needed; warm in microwave.

Helpful Hint
Purchase a 2-pound package of precooked bacon to keep in your freezer so you can add bits of bacon to omelets, sandwiches, salads, etc. (You can find precooked bacon in the meat section of the grocery store.) It is actually less expensive to buy bacon precooked than to cook it yourself, and you don't have to deal with the messy grease.

Cubed Ham

Yield: 10 cups cubed ham

Select a 5- to 6-pound precooked ham at your local grocery store and ask the butcher to cube it before you buy it. At home, place up to 2 cups cubed ham in several zip-top bags. Label and freeze to use for breakfast burritos, omelets, soups, and other dishes.

Spiral Cut Ham

Yield: 12 cups cubed ham

8-pound spiral-cut ham
2 cups honey
2 teaspoons dry mustard
1 teaspoon ground cloves

Preheat oven to 275°F. Place ham, cut side up, in a shallow pan with 2 cups water. Cover pan with foil and place in oven for 1 hour and 15 minutes.

Mix together the honey, mustard, and ground cloves, then pour evenly over the ham. Increase oven temperature to 425°F. Bake ham uncovered for 5 minutes, then remove from oven. This is a wonderful dish to serve to a large group of people or a great way to stock your freezer with delicious ham. I love to serve this dish with cheesy potatoes and red JELL-O salad.

Sweet Shredded Pork

Yield: 7 bags (4 servings each)

>   3- to 4-pound pork roast (any cut, the
>   more marbled the better)
>   1 bottle (2 liters) Dr. Pepper (Root Beer
>   and Pepsi also work)
>   1 can (14 ounces) pineapple tidbits,
>   undrained

Place pork roast in a slow cooker (for easy cleanup, don't forget to use a slow-cooker liner). Pour in Dr. Pepper and 1 can of pineapple with juice. Cook on LOW for 6 hours.

Do not open the lid during cooking, or you will need to increase the cooking time by 15 to 30 minutes.

Drain liquid (reserving 1 cup to freeze with the pork) and shred the pork roast in the slow cooker with two forks. Place leftover shredded pork in sandwich-size zip-top bags with 1 to 2 tablespoons liquid, then label and freeze.

To serve

Defrost in the microwave, pour off extra liquid, and serve over sweet beans and rice in a warm tortilla. Top with green chili sauce, salsa, and sour cream.

Cubed Chicken

Yield: 5 cups cubed chicken

Freeze 10 to 20 boneless skinless chicken breasts for an hour (or slightly defrost frozen chicken), then cube. (Slightly frozen chicken is easier to cube than raw or solidly frozen chicken.)

Place 4 cups of cubed chicken in each zip-top bag, then add a marinade (see "Emergency Substitutions" on page 19 for marinade ideas), then label and freeze.

For cooked, shredded chicken, see the recipe for roasted chicken. This is a great way to stock your freezer with cooked, shredded chicken that is very flavorful.

Browned Ground Beef

Yield: 7 to 8 sandwich-size bags of beef

> 2 large packages (4 pounds each) lean
>   ground beef
> 1 can (15 ounces) tomato sauce
> 3 tablespoons taco seasoning

Place 4 pounds ground beef in a large stockpot and add 2 cups water. Let meat cook until lightly browned, stirring occasionally.

Drain and cool beef, then place in sandwich-size zip-top freezer bags and label "browned beef."

Each freezer bag should hold about two cups.

Empty stockpot and add remaining 4 pounds ground beef plus 2 cups water. Let meat brown, stirring frequently. Drain liquid.

To the cooked beef in the stockpot, add tomato sauce and taco seasoning. Stir. Then add salt and pepper to taste. Let meat cool and place 2 to 3 cups taco meat in each of several zip-top plastic bags. Label "taco meat" and freeze.

Sirloin Strips

Yield: 7 to 8 sandwich-size bags of sirloin

> 2- to 3-pound beef roast (any cut, the
>   more marbled the better)

Marinade:
> ½ cups soy sauce
> 2 tablespoon rice wine vinegar
> 3 teaspoons baking soda
> 2 tablespoons cornstarch

To Freeze

Trim as much fat as possible from the beef. Then slice beef in thin strips against the grain (this makes the meat more tender). To save time, have your local butcher fajita-strip your roast. (This service should be free at the grocery store where you purchase the meat.) Place 1½ cups beef strips into each of several sandwich-size freezer bags, with the marinade equally dispersed inside. Lay meat flat to freeze so it will stack like bricks.

Turkey Breast

Buy two fully cooked turkey breasts, cube (or have the butcher do it), and then place 2 cups cubed turkey in each of several large freezer bags. Label and freeze.

Potatoes

Garlic Mashed Potatoes

Yield: 10 servings

5 pounds Yukon Gold potatoes (about 9
 large), peeled
2 tablespoons butter, softened
2 cups shredded cheddar cheese (or
 cheese of your choice)
6 ounces cream cheese, cubed
4 tablespoons creamed garlic (8 cloves,
 diced, crushed, and salted)
1¼ cups milk
2 to 3 tablespoons dried bacon bits, or 2
 ounces cooked bacon, crumbled
2 green onions, thinly chopped with
 scissors
2 tablespoons seasoned salt
salt and pepper to taste

Cut potatoes into 2-inch chunks and place in a large stockpot. Cover with water and bring to a boil. Reduce heat; cover and cook for 20 minutes or until tender. Drain.

In a large mixing bowl, mash potatoes with butter. Pour in milk and garlic, then beat in cream cheese, cheddar cheese, salt, seasoned salt, and pepper. Mix in bacon bits and chopped onion. Cool mashed potatoes. Freeze 2-cup portions in sandwich-size zip-top plastic bags for up to 2 months.

To serve
Thaw in refrigerator or defrost in microwave. Serve warm.

Onion Rings

Yield: 8 servings

2 eggs, beaten
1 cup milk
2 large onions, sliced
2 cups all-purpose flour
3 cups Italian-seasoned breadcrumbs
4 cups vegetable or canola oil

Place onions in freezer for 15 minutes to avoid crying when you cut them. While onions are in the freezer, set up 4 shallow dishes for dipping. In the first shallow dish, mix the egg and milk together and then pour half into the third dish. Place the flour in the second dish. Place the breadcrumbs in the fourth dish.

Cut each onion parallel to the root, making ½-inch slices. Separate the onion rings and then dip each into the egg mixture. Then dip onion ring in the flour, then in the egg mixture (third dish), and then in the breadcrumbs. Set on a paper towel until ready to fry.

Heat oil in a medium skillet to high heat (325°F). When oil is hot, place 8 to 10 onion rings in the oil and fry for 2 minutes on each side, or until they are golden brown. Place onion rings on a paper towel to soak up the grease. When cool, place onion rings on a baking sheet for 1 hour in the freezer. When frozen, place all onion rings in a large zip-top bag and use them as needed

To Serve
Place frozen onion rings on a baking sheet and bake at 425°F for 15 to 18 minutes. Or heat 2 cups oil in a skillet to 325°F and fry onion rings for 3 to 4 minutes. Serve warm with ketchup.

French Fries
Yield: 8 servings

    5 cups vegetable oil
    2 pounds baking potatoes

Pour oil in a deep fryer or heavy saucepan to reach halfway up the sides of the pan. Heat oil to 375°F. While oil heats, cut potatoes into uniformly sized sticks. As you work, put the cut potatoes in a bowl of cold water to keep them from turning brown and to release some of their starch.

Drain and dry potato sticks thoroughly to keep oil from splattering. Fry potatoes in batches so they don't stick together and so the oil temperature doesn't drop. Cook for 8 to 10 minutes until potatoes are a light golden color. Remove potatoes with a long-handled strainer and drain on brown paper sacks or paper towels. When fries are cool, place in freezer bags, label "oil 375°F, 5 minutes," and freeze.

To Serve
Bake fries at 425°F for 15 minutes (or until golden and crisp). Or heat oil to 375°F and return frozen french fries to oil in batches (have lid ready because the oil will splatter), cooking for 4 to 5 minutes or until golden and crispy. Drain on paper towels and sprinkle with seasoned salt. Serve immediately.

Vegetables

If you follow a few simple steps, you will find that vegetables are easy to freeze and will maintain a beautiful color and a great texture.

First, wash vegetables (broccoli, green beans, carrots, cauliflower, etc.) and place 6 to 8 cups water and 2 teaspoons salt in a large pot. Place the pot on the stove and turn heat to medium-high. Set out a strainer and a large bowl of ice water while you wait for the water to boil.

When water reaches a rolling boil, place vegetables in it for 1 to 2 minutes. Then pull them out using a strainer and immediately place them in ice water. The ice water stops the cooking process and leaves the vegetables bright and crisp, but not overcooked.

Once vegetables have been blanched, you can add flavor by sautéing them in seasoned chicken broth. To do this, place 1 cup of chicken broth in a skillet and stir in some dried herbs (rosemary thyme, basil, etc.). Add vegetables and cook, stirring constantly, for 1 to 2 minutes or until the color brightens. Remove vegetables from pan and cool. Package vegetables in zip-top bags, then label and freeze. To serve, simply remove packaging and reheat in a microwave or in a toaster oven.

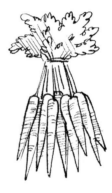

Fried Green Beans
Yield: 10 servings

2 eggs, beaten
1 cup milk
11 ounces fresh green beans
2 cups all-purpose flour
1 tablespoon garlic salt
2 cups breadcrumbs
4 cups vegetable or canola oil

Wash and trim green beans. Set up 4 shallow dishes for dipping. In the first bowl, mix together the egg and milk, and then pour half into the third bowl. In the second bowl, place the flour and garlic salt. In the fourth bowl, place the breadcrumbs.

Heat oil in a medium skillet to high heat (325°F). Do not use olive oil, as it will burn at high temperatures.

First, coat the beans in the egg–milk mixture, then the flour mixture, then the egg–milk mixture (third dish). Then roll the beans in the breadcrumbs until they are completely covered. Place the dipped beans on a paper towel.

When the oil is hot, fry the beans in bunches for 2 minutes or until golden brown. Drain on paper towels, and sprinkle with salt. Serve warm with the chilled wasabi-cucumber ranch sauce (see recipe below), or freeze for later.

To Freeze
Place fried green beans on a baking sheet and freeze for 1 hour. Then place green beans in a large zip-top bag and freeze.

To Serve
Heat oven to 425°F and place frozen fried green beans on a foil-covered baking sheet. Bake for 10 minutes or until green beans are golden brown and warmed through. Serve with the chilled wasabi-cucumber ranch sauce.

Wasabi-Cucumber Ranch Sauce
Yield: 1 cup sauce

½ cup ranch dressing
1 cucumber, peeled and seeded
2 tablespoons salad dressing (I use Miracle Whip)
2 teaspoons prepared horseradish
1 teaspoon apple cider vinegar
2 teaspoons wasabi paste
¼ cup cilantro
salt and pepper to taste

To Serve Wasabi-Cucumber Ranch Sauce
On serving day, make the dip by combining all of the ingredients in a blender on high speed until smooth. Cover and chill. Dip will thicken as it chills. This dip does not freeze well, so make it fresh when you serve the fried green beans. Store dip in refrigerator and use within 7 days.

Beans and Rice

Cooked Rice

Yield: 6 cups cooked rice

4 cups uncooked white or brown rice
5 to 6 cups water (or chicken or beef
    broth)

The general rule for fluffy, sticky white rice is to cook 1 cup of rice in 1¼ cups water. I measure the amount of water by first pouring the rice in the rice cooker, then adding enough water so that with my pointer finger I touch the top of the rice and the water comes up to my first knuckle.

Brown rice requires another ½ cup water and an extra 10 to 15 minutes of cooking time.

Both brown rice and white rice freeze well. After rice has cooked, simply scoop 2 to 3 cups into a sandwich-size zip-top bag. Freeze flat so you can stack the bags of rice like bricks to maximize freezer space.

To Serve

Heat frozen rice (in zip-top bag or a covered microwavable dish) in the microwave on HIGH for 4 to 5 minutes. The ice crystals in the rice will steam the rice and it will be moist and fluffy.

Refried Beans

Yield: 10 cups refried beans

2 onions, peeled and chopped
6 cups dried pinto beans, rinsed
1 fresh jalapeno pepper, seeded and
    chopped (optional)
1 cup crumbled bacon (optional)
3 tablespoons minced garlic
1 tablespoon salt
3 teaspoons fresh ground pepper
½ teaspoon ground cumin
16 to 18 cups water (for more flavor, use
    half unsalted chicken broth and half
    water)
salt and pepper to taste

Place onions, rinsed beans, jalapeno, garlic, salt, pepper, and cumin in a slow cooker. Pour in water and stir to combine. Cook on HIGH for 8 hours.

Once the beans are cooked, beat them in the slow cooker with an electric beater, adding water as needed to attain desired consistency.

When beans have cooled, add salt and pepper to taste and place in freezer bags, then label and freeze.

To Serve

Defrost beans and serve with chips or as a side dish to a chimichanga dinner.

Helpful Hint

To make a delicious bean dip, mix half the mashed refried beans with 2 cups salsa, 4 cups shredded cheese, 8 ounces cream cheese, 16 ounces sour cream, 2 tablespoons chili powder, and ½ teaspoon ground cumin. Mix in slow cooker and cook for 2 hours so flavors can fuse. Freeze leftovers.

Sweet Beans and Rice

Yield: 4 to 6 servings

2 cans (14½ ounces each) black beans, drained
6 cups frozen cooked rice
½ cup sugar

Warm rice in microwave for 1 to 2 minutes. In a skillet on the stove, mix together beans, rice, and sugar. Stir until well mixed and warm.

To Serve

Defrost sweet beans and rice and add to burritos or serve as a side dish.

Tofu

If you place an unopened package of tofu in the freezer without draining it, the tofu will be crumbly and have a soft consistency when defrosted. Tofu frozen this way works well as a substitute for ricotta cheese in Italian dishes.

If you want the tofu to be firm when you defrost it, remove the wrapping and drain the water from the container. Then set the tofu on a plate that is covered with several layers of paper towels. Place a few more paper towels on top of the tofu and gently press to soak up the moisture. Place something heavy on top of the towel-covered tofu and let sit for 15 to 30 minutes.

Once the tofu has drained, place it in a zip-top bag, then label and freeze.

To Serve
Simply defrost the tofu in the refrigerator or microwave, and use it as your recipe directs. Because it was frozen, the tofu may take on a yellow tinge, but the taste is still perfectly normal.

Sauces and Stock

Spaghetti Sauce

Yield: 13 cups sauce

2 onions, diced
2 teaspoons garlic, minced
1 cup crumbled bacon
2 pounds Italian sausage
2 pounds browned hamburger
1 extra-large can (106 ounces) tomato
    sauce, or 4 large cans (28 ounces
    each) spaghetti sauce
1 extra-large can (106 ounces) diced
    tomatoes, or 4 large cans (28 ounces
    each) Italian-style diced tomatoes,
    undrained
4 cans (2.4 ounces each) sliced black
    olives (optional)
3 tablespoons Italian seasoning (or use
    oregano and garlic salt)
2 tablespoons dried basil
salt and pepper to taste

Over medium-high heat, cook onions, garlic, sausage, and hamburger until onions are soft and the meat is no longer pink. Remove pan from heat and drain the grease.

Place meat back in pot and add tomato sauce, diced tomatoes, olives, and seasonings. Stir just until combined, then cool and place 4 cups in each large zip-top bag. Then label and freeze flat.

This sauce can be defrosted and used for spaghetti, lasagna, manicotti, ravioli, or pizza. Once the sauce is defrosted, pour off the extra liquid.

Helpful Hint

Don't cry! To avoid the acidic reaction that can happen in your eyes when you cut a fresh onion, freeze the onion for at least 15 minutes before cutting it. Also, for easy dicing, don't cut off the root of the onion. Instead, cut the onion in half through the root, and in a grid-like pattern using the lines on the onion, make slices. The root will hold the onion together while you dice it. Then cut crossways up the onion for perfect dicing.

Chicken Stock

Yield: 8 cups stock

> leftover chicken bones and skin
> 2 celery stalks
> 1 onion, quartered
> 2 carrots
> 2 tablespoons chopped fresh parsley
> ½ teaspoon salt
> ¼ teaspoon pepper
> 8 cups water

Put chicken bones and skin into a large stockpot and cover with cold water. Add celery, onion, carrots, parsley, salt, and pepper.

Bring to a boil and immediately reduce heat to bring the stock to barely a simmer. Simmer uncovered at least 4 hours, occasionally skimming off the foam that comes to the surface.

Remove the bones and skin and strain the stock. If making stock for soup, you may want to reduce the stock by simmering it a few hours longer. This will make it more concentrated and therefore easier to store.

Once the stock cools, freeze it in cupcake pans for a quick ½-cup measurement, or freeze large amounts in zip-top plastic bags. To freeze in cupcake pans, line the pans with plastic wrap, pour in chicken stock, and freeze for 1 to 2 hours. After stock has frozen, pop it out of the cupcake pan, place the "cubes" a large zip-top bag, and store in the freezer. Use the chicken stock in soups, as the cooking liquid for rice, etc.

Muffins and Breads

Muffins

Mix-and-Match Muffin Mix

Yield: 24 muffins

2 cups all-purpose flour
1½ teaspoons baking powder
½ teaspoon baking soda
½ teaspoon ground cinnamon
½ teaspoon salt
2 eggs, beaten
1¼ cups filling (choose from list below)
1 cup nuts or seeds (optional)
1 cup sugar
½ cup cooking oil

Filling (do not use dried fruit)
Apples, diced
Applesauce
Apricots, chopped
Bananas, mashed
Berries
Carrots, grated

Cherries, pitted and chopped
Lemon juice (only add ⅓ cup)
Oranges, chopped
Orange juice (only add ⅓ cup)
Peaches, chopped
Pears, chopped
Pumpkin, canned (add 2 teaspoons
    pumpkin-pie spice)
Strawberries (well drained)
Zucchini, grated

*Some delicious combinations are carrot raisin walnut, cranberry orange, and pumpkin raisin sunflower seed.

Preheat oven to 375°F. In a large bowl, combine the dry ingredients. Make a well in the center of the flour mixture and set aside.

In a separate medium bowl, combine the remaining (wet) ingredients. Stir wet mixture into flour mixture just until moistened. (Batter should be lumpy.)

Place paper muffin-cup liners close together on a large baking sheet so the sides touch. Spoon batter into the paper liners until they are ⅔ full.

Place the baking sheet in the freezer for 1 hour. Then place the frozen muffin cups in a large zip-top bag and freeze.

To Serve

When you are ready to use the muffins, take them out of the freezer and place them in a muffin pan, then bake at 350°F for 20 minutes.

White Chocolate-Chip Macadamia-Nut Muffins

Yield: 24 muffins

3½ cups all-purpose flour
1½ cups sugar
1½ tablespoons baking powder
1 teaspoon salt
½ cup (1 stick) butter, melted
2 eggs
1 cup milk
1 bag (12 ounces) white chocolate chips
1 small bag (4 ounces) macadamia nuts, chopped

In a large bowl, mix the flour, sugar, baking powder, and salt.

In a medium bowl, whisk together the butter, eggs, and milk. Stir into the dry mixture until moistened. Fold in the chips and nuts.

Fill paper-lined muffin cups ⅔ full with batter. Bake at 400°F for 15 to 18 minutes or until a toothpick inserted in the center comes out clean. Cool for 5 minutes before removing from the pan, then transfer to a wire rack. When muffins are cool, glaze them ½ cup white, semisweet, or milk chocolate chips, melted, combine with 2 tablespoons heavy whipping cream. Then place muffins in a zip-top freezer bag, and freeze.

To Serve

Defrost muffins on HIGH in the microwave for 10 seconds.

Cherry Cheesecake Muffins

Yield: 21 regular muffins or 6 jumbo muffins

⅓ cup (5½ tablespoons) butter, softened
¾ cup sugar
2 eggs
1½ cups all-purpose flour

1½ teaspoons baking powder
1 teaspoon ground cinnamon
⅓ cup milk

Cream Cheese Filling
6 ounces cream cheese, softened
⅓ cup sugar
1 egg
1½ cups fresh or frozen cherries (or any
    type of berries)

Streusel Topping
¼ cup all-purpose flour
¼ cup brown sugar, firmly packed
½ teaspoon ground cinnamon
1 tablespoon cold butter

In a large mixing bowl, cream butter and sugar. Add eggs; beat well. Combine flour, baking powder, and cinnamon; add to creamed mixture alternately with milk. Fill greased or paper-lined muffin cups ⅓ full.

For filling, in a small mixing bowl, beat cream cheese, sugar, and egg until smooth. Fold in berries. Drop a rounded tablespoonful into the center of each muffin.

For topping, combine flour, brown sugar, and cinnamon in a small bowl; cut in butter until crumbly. Sprinkle over batter. (Muffin cups will be full.)

To Serve
Bake at 375°F for 25 to 30 minutes or until a toothpick inserted in the center comes out clean. Cool for 5 minutes before removing from pans and transferring to wire racks. Serve warm. Refrigerate leftovers. For quicker muffins, freeze baked muffins on paper plates and wrap in plastic. Simply defrost muffins in microwave (10 to 20 seconds on HIGH) and serve warm.

To Freeze
Fill greased or paper-lined muffin cups ⅓ full with batter, then add filling and topping. Place muffin tray in freezer for 1 hour. Then place muffins in a large zip-top bag. Label "375°F, 30 minutes," and use as needed. To serve, bake uncooked frozen muffins in preheated 375°F oven for 30 minutes or until a toothpick comes out clean.

Breads

Banana Bread with Streusel Topping

Yield: 2 loaves

    2 cups all-purpose flour
    1½ teaspoons baking powder
    ½ teaspoon baking soda
    ½ teaspoon ground cinnamon
    pinch salt
    2 eggs, beaten
    1½ cups mashed bananas (about 3
        medium bananas)
    1 cup sugar
    ½ cup cooking oil or applesauce

Spray two loaf pans with cooking spray and set aside. In a large bowl, combine dry ingredients. Make a well in the center of the flour mixture; set aside.

In a separate medium bowl, combine the wet ingredients. Stir into flour mixture until just moistened; batter should be lumpy.

Spoon batter into greased loaf pans. Mix the streusel topping and sprinkle it over batter.

Streusel Topping

In a small bowl, mix ½ cup flour and ½ cup packed brown sugar. Using a fork or pastry blender, cut in 3 tablespoons cold butter until mixture becomes crumbly.

Bake at 350°F for 55 minutes or until a toothpick inserted in center comes out clean. Cool in pan for 10 minutes, and then cool on a wire rack. Freeze one loaf and serve the other.

Chocolate-Chunk Pumpkin Bread

Yield: 2 loaves

    4 cups all-purpose flour
    4 teaspoons baking powder
    1 teaspoon baking soda
    2 teaspoons salt
    2 teaspoons ground cinnamon
    1 teaspoon ground nutmeg
    4 eggs
    2 cups mashed, cooked pumpkin
    2 cups sugar

1 cup packed brown sugar, firmly
   packed
1 cup milk
½ cup vegetable oil or applesauce
2 cups chocolate chips or 6 squares
   semisweet baking chocolate,
   coarsely chopped

Mix flour, baking powder, baking soda, salt, and spices until well blended; set aside.

In a bowl, beat eggs. Add remaining ingredients except chocolate, mixing with a wire whisk until well blended.

Blend dry mixture with wet mixture and mix thoroughly. Fold in chocolate.

Pour into 2 greased 9 x 5-inch loaf pans. Bake at 350°F for 55 minutes to 1 hour or until toothpick inserted in center comes out clean.

Cool bread in pans for 10 minutes, then remove from pans and cool completely on wire rack. Serve immediately or freeze each loaf in a large zip-top bag for up to 3 months.

Zucchini Bread

Yield: 2 loaves (or 1 loaf and 12 muffins)

6 cups all-purpose flour
4 teaspoons ground cinnamon
2 teaspoons baking soda
2 teaspoons salt
1 teaspoon baking powder
1 teaspoon ground nutmeg
4 eggs, beaten
3 cups sugar
4 cups finely shredded, unpeeled
   zucchini
1 cup applesauce (or cooking oil)

Grease two 8 x 4 x 2-inch loaf pans and set aside. In a medium bowl, mix dry ingredients. Make a well in the center of the flour mixture and set aside.

In another medium bowl, combine eggs, sugar, zucchini, and oil. Add the wet ingredients to the flour mixture and stir until just moistened (batter should be lumpy). To make muffins, fill paper-lined muffin cups ⅔ full with batter. Bake at 375°F for 15 minutes or until a toothpick inserted in the center comes out clean.

To make loaves, divide batter into 2 loaf pans. Bake at 350°F for 50 to 55 minutes or until a toothpick inserted in the center comes out clean. (The time and temperature remain the same if you are cooking 1 loaf of bread.) Cool in pan for 10 minutes, then remove from pan and cool on a wire rack. Place in a large zip-top bag and freeze.

To Serve

Prepare the maple frosting and spread on bread. Serve chilled.

Maple Frosting

Yield: ½ cup frosting (enough for 1 loaf zucchini bread)

> 3 tablespoons brown sugar
> 2 tablespoons hot water
> 2 tablespoons (¼ stick) butter
> 1 teaspoon vanilla
> 3 cups powdered sugar

Combine brown sugar and hot water. Add butter and vanilla, then mix in powdered sugar. Spread on top of zucchini bread.

Cinnamon Rolls

Yield: 3 dozen large rolls

> 4 tablespoons yeast
> 4 cups warm milk
> 1 cup sugar
> 4 teaspoons salt
> 1 cup shortening
> 4 eggs
> 12 cups all-purpose flour

Cinnamon Topping
> 3 cups brown sugar, firmly packed, divided
> 2 tablespoons cinnamon
> 1 cup chopped nuts (optional)
> 1 cup (2 sticks) margarine or butter, softened

In a bowl, thoroughly combine the cinnamon with 1½ cups brown sugar; stir in chopped nuts.

Warm 4 cups milk in the microwave for 1 to 2 minutes. Mix together all remaining dough ingredients except 6 cups flour. Gradually stir in remaining flour, adding a little more if the dough sticks to your fingers. (The dough will be different depending on the humidity, so simply add flour until the dough is no longer sticky.)

On a lightly floured countertop, roll the dough into a long rectangle (about 16 by 20 inches). Spread softened margarine on the dough, then sprinkle the cinnamon topping over the margarine. Top with remaining 1½ cups brown sugar.

Starting at the long edge of the rectangle, roll up the dough like a burrito so that the cinnamon topping is inside. Pinch the edges closed.

With a knife, lightly mark the dough in 1-inch sections. Then, using a sharp knife, cut into pieces. Place each cinnamon roll, cut side up, on a baking sheet.

To Serve
Let cinnamon rolls rise for 30 minutes, then bake at 375°F for 15 minutes. Alternately, rolls can be covered loosely with plastic wrap (sprayed with cooking spray) and refrigerated overnight, then baked in the morning.

To Freeze
Place uncooked cinnamon rolls on a baking sheet in the freezer for 1 hour. Then place them in a large zip-top bag and freeze. To serve, place frozen rolls on a baking sheet and cover them loosely with plastic wrap. Let rolls rise overnight. In the morning, remove plastic wrap and bake rolls at 375°F for 15 minutes.

To make fruit-flavored cinnamon rolls, simply butter the dough, then spread on jam or marmalade (any flavor works—strawberry, raspberry, orange, etc.) before sprinkling with cinnamon sugar. Then roll the dough and slice.

Cream Cheese Frosting
Yield: frosting for 12 large cinnamon rolls

> 2 tablespoons (¼ stick) butter
> 6 ounces (¾ cup) cream cheese, softened
> 2 teaspoons vanilla
> 4 cups powdered sugar

In a small bowl, combine first three ingredients, beating on low speed until creamy. Gradually add sugar until fluffy. If necessary, add milk to make frosting easier to spread. Do not freeze the frosting, because it tends to separate and crystallize.

Wheat Bread

Yield: 5 loaves (or 4 loaves and 1 pizza crust)

5 cups warm water
1 cup honey
1 cup olive, canola, or vegetable oil
2 tablespoons yeast
¼ cup gluten
1 cup hot water
9 cups whole-wheat flour
9 cups all-purpose flour
1½ tablespoons salt
1 cup sunflower seeds (optional)

Heat 5 cups water in the microwave for 1 to 2 minutes. Pour the warm water, oil, and honey into a large mixer and blend. Add yeast, gluten, and 1 cup hot water, then wheat flour. Add 1 cup all-purpose flour and mix for 5 minutes. Add the salt and the sunflower seeds.

This dough can be different each time you make the bread, depending on the humidity, so if the dough sticks to your fingers, add more flour.

Preheat oven on lowest setting. When dough is ready, place it on a greased counter and shape it into a big circle. Next, cut the dough into five sections with a knife.

Shape each dough section into a long, oval shape and place each in a greased bread pan. I like to make 4 loaves of bread and use the last piece of dough for a pizza. To make the pizza crust, roll the dough flat, fold over the edges, and poke the dough all over with a fork. Then let it rise with the bread for 25 minutes. Add toppings and bake pizza at 425°F for 15 to 18 minutes or until cheese has melted and is golden brown.

Let bread dough rise in a warm oven for 25 minutes. Then bake loaves at 350°F for 30 to 35 minutes. Butter the top of each loaf and let bread rest for 10 minutes. Remove loaves from pans and cool on wire racks. Freeze in bread bags or large zip-top bags.

To Serve

Defrost bread for 1 minute on HIGH in the microwave, or let the bread defrost on the counter. When dried, this bread makes excellent French toast or a great stuffing mix.

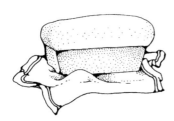

White Bread

Yield: 4 loaves (or 4 large pizzas)

12 cups all-purpose flour
1 tablespoon salt
3 tablespoons instant or rapid-rise yeast
½ cup sugar
2 tablespoons dough enhancer
2 tablespoons gluten (optional)
½ cup canola or vegetable oil
4 cups warm water

In a large mixer, combine flour, salt, yeast, sugar, dough enhancer, and gluten.

In a glass measuring cup, warm the water in the microwave for 1 minute. Gradually add the water and oil to the flour mixture.

When combined, let the dough mix for 2 minutes. Add more flour if the dough is too sticky, more water if too dry. Let the mixer knead the dough for 8 minutes. This will ensure that the bread will rise.

Preheat oven on the lowest setting. When the dough is ready, place it on a lightly oiled countertop. Shape the dough into a big circle, then cut into four sections with a knife. To make bread loaves, shape each dough section into a long oval and place in a greased bread pan. Let rise in a warm oven for 30 minutes.

Bake at 350°F for 25 minutes. Remove loaves from pans, butter the tops, and cool on a wire rack. Freeze in bread bags or large zip-top freezer bags.

To make 4 pizzas crusts, roll dough into large, flat circles and fold over the edges. Poke dough with a fork and bake on a baking sheet at 500°F for 3 to 4 minutes. When cool, wrap in layers of plastic wrap, and freeze.

For baking directions, see the Pizza Dough recipe on page 48. For sauce, see the Pizza Sauce recipe on page 49.

To Serve
Defrost bread in the microwave for 1 minute on HIGH, or defrost on the countertop.

Roll Dough
Yield: 30 rolls

   2 tablespoons instant or rapid-rise yeast
   ½ cup warm water
   2 cups milk
   1 cup shortening or Butter Flavor Crisco
   ¾ cup sugar
   2 eggs
   ½ cup cold water
   2 teaspoons salt
   8 cups all-purpose flour (use half wheat
      and half all-purpose flour for more
      nutritious rolls)

In a bread mixer or large mixing bowl, mix yeast in ½ cup warm water. Let sit for 5 minutes.

In a glass measuring cup, heat 2 cups milk for 2 minutes in the microwave. Add shortening. Pour milk mixture into yeast mixture in bread mixer or mixing bowl.

Add sugar, eggs, salt, and ½ cup cold water. Mix with a wire whisk until well combined. Using a dough hook, mix 3 cups flour into the yeast mixture. Mix salt into 1 cup flour. Add the flour—salt mixture 1 cup at a time until the dough lightly sticks to your fingers. You may need more flour depending on the humidity.

Split the dough into two sections and place in 2 large greased bowls. Cover bowls with greased plastic and set in a warm place to let rise until doubled in size. (I usually turn the oven to WARM [170°F] for 5 min. Then I turn off the oven and place the bowls on the middle rack.) You can freeze half the dough in zip-top bags to be used later for scones, bread bowls, pizza crusts, etc.

To Make Rolls
After the dough has doubled in size, punch it down and place it on a lightly oiled counter. Roll out the dough in a large circle, then spread it with butter.

Cut the dough into 3-inch triangles. Starting at the wide end, roll each triangle, moving towards the tip of the triangle, creating a crescent shape.

Set rolls on a lightly greased and floured cookie sheet, cover with a towel, and let rise for 30 minutes. Be careful not to move the pan while dough is rising or the rolls may lose their shape.

Bake at 375°F for 8 or 9 minutes, or until rolls are golden on top. To prevent rolls from getting sticky on the bottom, cool them on a wire rack. Then place rolls in zip-top plastic bags and put them in the freezer.

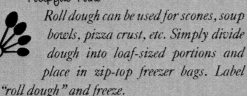

Helpful Hint
Roll dough can be used for scones, soup bowls, pizza crust, etc. Simply divide dough into loaf-sized portions and place in zip-top freezer bags. Label "roll dough" and freeze.

Scones

Yield: 8 to 10 scones

8 to 10 freezer rolls, prepared and frozen
3 cups vegetable or canola oil
powdered sugar, butter, or honey (if desired)

Pour 2 to 3 inches of oil into a large skillet. Heat to medium-high setting or 375°F. Flatten each dinner roll into a 3- to 4-inch circle.

When oil is hot, drop in dough pieces one at a time. When one side of scone is golden brown, flip it over (cook for about 15 seconds each side). Remove from hot oil and drain on a paper towel.

Serve hot. Sprinkle with powdered sugar, or serve with butter or honey.

Indian Tacos

For quick Indian tacos, serve scones with refried beans, browned ground beef, shredded cheese, chopped lettuce, chopped tomatoes, cilantro, and sour cream.

Bread Bowls

Yield: 3 bread bowls

1 loaf frozen bread dough, thawed but still cold
1 egg white (discard yolk)
sesame seeds (optional)

Cut loaf into thirds. Form each third into a ball. Place on a greased cookie sheet. Brush with egg whites and sprinkle sesame seeds on top. Let rise until double in size.

Bake at 350°F for 25 minutes, or until golden brown. Cool and slice off the top. Hollow out bread and fill with dip, chili, or soup. For larger bowls, divide dough in half instead of thirds.

Wrap leftover bread bowls in plastic wrap, place in a large zip-top bag, and freeze for 3 to 6 months.

To Serve
Defrost frozen bread bowls on the countertop at room temperature or for 30 seconds in the microwave on HIGH. Fill with warm soup, chili, or dip.

Pizza Dough
Yield: crust for three 14-inch pizzas

12 cups all-purpose flour
1 tablespoon salt
3 tablespoons instant yeast
½ cup sugar
2 tablespoons dough enhancer (optional)
½ cup canola or vegetable oil
4 cups warm water

1 tablespoon oregano
½ tablespoon garlic powder

In a large mixer, combine the flour, salt, yeast, sugar, and dough enhancer.

In a glass measuring cup, warm the water in the microwave for 2 minutes. Gradually, add the water and oil to the flour mixture. When combined, let the dough mix for 2 minutes. Dough should be elastic and should not stick to your fingers. Add more flour if too sticky, more water if too dry.

Let the mixer knead the dough for 8 minutes. (The dough may be frozen at this point. Just place each piece in a large freezer zip-top bag, then label and freeze. To use, simply defrost in the microwave for 1 minute on HIGH and roll out dough to make a pizza, stromboli, or calzone.)

Preheat oven to 500°F. Place pizza stone (best for a crispy crust) in the oven while it is heating up. Or grease a large pizza pan.

Shape dough into a large circle, then cut it into three sections with a knife. Lightly oil countertop and roll out each pizza crust with a rolling pin. Fold over the edges and press down to form a crust. With a fork, pierce pizza dough every inch or two to reduce the number of bubbles in the crust.

Sprinkle cornmeal or flour on the pizza pan and place pizza dough on pan by folding over half the dough on your forearm and then lifting dough onto pizza pan.

Bake each pizza crust for 4 minutes at 500°F. You can freeze the crust at this point (when cooled) or continue with toppings.

Remove hot crust from oven and **top with ½ cup cheese first** (this will keep the frozen pizza from getting soggy).

Prepare pizza sauce (recipe follows) and pour sauce on top of cheese. Pile on desired toppings; top again with cheese.

Cool pizza and then wrap it in plastic wrap without the pan. Label "500°F, 10 to 15 minutes" and freeze.

To Serve

Do not defrost frozen pizza. Remove plastic wrap. Place pizza on a pizza stone dusted with cornmeal, or on an aluminum pan in the oven while it is preheating to 500°F. Bake for 10 to 15 minutes or until cheese is melted and crust is golden.

Pizza Sauce

Yield: 3½ cups sauce (enough for three 14-inch pizzas)

1 large can (29 ounces) tomato sauce
3 tablespoons oregano
3 teaspoons minced garlic

Open can of tomato sauce and add oregano and garlic to the can. Stir carefully so it will not spill. Pour about ⅓ of sauce (just over 1 cup) onto pizza crust. Divide remaining sauce in half and freeze in zip-top freezer bags.

Helpful Hint

A great way to save money on pizza toppings is to buy them in bulk. You can purchase extra-large bags of toppings like pepperoni and shredded cheese, and large cans of toppings like pineapple and olives. For each topping, place 2 cups in each of several zip-top plastic bags, then label each bag. Place bags in a larger zip-top bag before freezing so the smaller bags stay together in the freezer. Pull out as needed and thaw in microwave.

Fococcia Bread (Italian Pull-Apart Bread)

Yield: 2 loaves (8 servings each)

2 tablespoons active dry yeast
2 teaspoons sugar
3 cups all-purpose flour
2 teaspoons salt
¼ cup chopped fresh rosemary (or
    3 teaspoons dried rosemary)
2 teaspoons garlic powder
2 tablespoons plus 2 teaspoons
    olive oil
1¼ cup warm water

Preheat oven to 450°F. Spray a cookie sheet and sprinkle with cornmeal.

In a medium bowl, combine yeast, sugar, flour, salt, and herbs. Add water and oil. Mix by hand or in a large mixer until the dough forms a pliable ball. Knead for 10 minutes.

Divide dough into two balls and flatten on cookie sheet. Spread evenly until dough forms an 8-inch circle that is ¼ inch thick.

Press dough with fingertips to make dimples; sprinkle with rosemary and salt. Drizzle evenly with olive oil and grind fresh pepper over all.

Bake for 15 minutes until crisp and golden. Eat right away or freeze in large zip-top plastic bags for 3 to 6 months.

To Serve

Warm in microwave for 30 seconds. Dip pieces of bread into a small dish of balsamic vinegar mixed with olive oil, salt, and fresh ground pepper.

Breadstick Twists

Yield: 2 dozen breadsticks

3 cups all-purpose flour
½ tablespoon salt
1½ tablespoons instant yeast
¼ cup sugar
1 tablespoon dough enhancer
1 tablespoon gluten (optional)
¼ cup canola or vegetable oil
2 cups warm water
24 wooden skewers

Combine flour, salt, yeast, sugar, dough enhancer, and gluten.

In a glass liquid measuring cup, warm the water in the microwave for 1 minute. Add the oil to the water mixture and pour onto the flour mixture. When combined, mix the dough for 2 minutes. Add more flour if dough is too sticky, more water if dry. Let mixer knead the dough for 8 minutes so that bread will rise properly.

On greased countertop, roll dough into a large rectangle, and, using a knife or pizza cutter, slice into 1-inch strips.

Wrap dough strips around the skewers (leaving 3 inches at the bottom of the skewer for a handhold) and place on a greased cookie sheet. Repeat with remaining dough.

Place cookie sheet in the freezer for 1 hour or until dough is frozen. Then wrap breadsticks in plastic wrap or place in large zip-top freezer bags until ready to serve.

To Serve
Place frozen breadsticks on a greased cookie sheet and let them rise overnight. Or set them out to rise a few hours before needed. When they have doubled in size, preheat oven to 375°F. Bake twists at 375°F for 12 to 15 minutes or until golden brown. While breadsticks bake, make breadstick topping (recipe follows). Do not brush on the seasoning until after breadsticks are baked. Remove from oven and brush with the butter seasoning. Serve breadsticks warm standing up in a large vase.

Breadstick Topping
    6 tablespoons melted butter
    ½ teaspoon garlic salt
    ½ teaspoon garlic powder
    ½ teaspoon dill weed
    ¼ teaspoon Italian seasoning

Mix all ingredients together. Brush on baked breadstick twists while they are hot.

Crunchy Parmesan Breadsticks
Yield: 24 breadsticks

    24 large frozen rolls, thawed but still
        cold
    ½ cup (1 stick) butter or margarine,
        melted
    ½ cup shredded or grated Parmesan
        cheese
    garlic salt
    dried parsley

Shape frozen rolls into 24 six-inch football-shaped breadsticks. Pour melted butter on a large baking sheet. Roll each breadstick in butter until completely coated.

Place Parmesan cheese in a separate bowl and roll each buttered breadstick in the cheese. Place breadsticks on a foil-covered baking sheet and sprinkle with garlic salt and parsley.

Cover with greased plastic wrap. At this point, you can freeze the breadsticks or bake them and freeze the leftovers. (See "To Freeze," below.) To continue baking, place breadsticks in a warm oven (heated to 170°F and then turned off). Let rise until double in size. Remove plastic wrap and bake at 350°F for 20 minutes or until golden brown.

To Freeze

If you want to freeze the breadsticks before letting them rise, place them on a baking sheet in the freezer for 1 hour. Then put them in a large zip-top bag and freeze. When ready to use, bake as directed above at 350°F for 20 minutes.

You can also freeze baked breadsticks in a zip-top plastic bag for up to 2 months.

To Serve

Bake frozen, uncooked breadsticks on a foil-covered baking sheet at 350°F for 20 minutes. Or defrost frozen, baked rolls on countertop, or thaw in microwave for 10 to 20 seconds.

Cheesy Pull-Aparts

Yield: 15 breadsticks

> 1 pound frozen bread dough
> 3 to 4 cups shredded mozzarella
>   cheese
> 4 tablespoons olive oil
> 2 tablespoons oregano

Pizza Sauce for Breadsticks
> 2 small cans (8 ounces each) tomato
>   sauce
> 2 tablespoons oregano
> 2 teaspoons minced garlic

In a medium bowl, mix together tomato sauce, oregano, and garlic. When ready to serve, heat sauce.

Preheat oven to WARM (about 170°F). Grease a large baking sheet.

Defrost frozen dough in the microwave for 20 seconds or until pliable. Roll dough into a 9 x 15-inch rectangle; place dough on greased baking sheet. Sprinkle cheese over lower half of the rectangle. Fold dough lengthwise over the cheese; pinch to seal edges. Turn oven off, cover the dough, and place in the warm oven to rise until doubled (about 30 minutes.)

Uncover dough and turn oven to 375°F. Bake for 18 to 20 minutes or until golden brown. Move from baking sheet to wire rack and cool for at least 10 minutes. Brush top of dough with olive oil, then sprinkle with dried oregano. Cut crosswise into fifteen 1-inch breadsticks. Serve warm with pizza sauce or ranch dressing and freeze the leftovers in a large zip-top bag.

Cornbread

Yield: two 8-inch square pans (6 servings each)

    1 cup all-purpose flour
    ¾ cup cornmeal
    2 to 3 tablespoons sugar
    2½ teaspoons baking powder
    ¾ teaspoon salt
    2 eggs, beaten
    1 cup milk

    ½ cup sour cream
    ¼ cup cooking oil or melted butter
    ½ cup canned or frozen corn (optional)

Preheat oven to 400°F. In a medium bowl, mix together flour, cornmeal, sugar, baking powder, and salt; set aside.

Spray two 8-inch pans with cooking spray. In a small bowl, combine eggs, milk, sour cream, oil, and corn. Add egg mixture all at once to flour mixture. Stir just until moistened.

Pour batter into pans. Bake for 15 to 20 minutes or until a wooden toothpick inserted in center comes out clean. Serve warm with butter and honey.

To Freeze
After bread cools, slice into squares and place on a paper plate in a large zip-top freezer bag.

To Serve
Defrost cornbread in microwave for 20 to 30 seconds and serve warm with butter and honey.

Breakfast

Breakfast Egg Sandwiches

Yield: 12 sandwiches

12 English muffins
½ cup milk
12 eggs
24 precooked bacon strips (can
        substitute Canadian bacon, or
        cooked sausage patties)
12 slices cheese

Butter muffins (or spread with olive oil), then place on a baking sheet and toast in a 350°F oven for 4 minutes.

Crack 12 eggs into a large skillet on medium-high heat and beat with a wire whisk. Add ½ cup milk and seasoned salt to taste. Continue to stir just until all liquid is gone and eggs are scrambled. Remove from heat promptly to prevent eggs from drying out.

If desired, spread Miracle Whip or mayonnaise on the muffin. Assemble sandwiches with 1 English muffin, 1 scoop of scrambled eggs, 2 strips of bacon, and 1 slice of cheese.

Wrap each sandwich individually in plastic, then place several sandwiches in a large zip-top freezer bag.

To Serve

Remove sandwich from bag, then remove plastic wrap and microwave on HIGH for 45 seconds. Turn sandwich over and microwave on HIGH for another 45 seconds, or until warm. Or to bake, remove wrappings, line a pan with foil, and bake sandwiches at 400°F for 10 to 15 minutes.

Breakfast Burritos

Yield: 24 burritos

18 eggs, beaten
2 tablespoons milk
2 teaspoons seasoned salt, or salt and
        pepper to taste
1 pound sausage (cubed ham and/or
        crumbled bacon will also work)
1 cup chunky salsa
3 cups cheddar cheese, shredded
24 large flour tortillas

Cook sausage in a large skillet with ¼ cup water until it is fully cooked and the water has evaporated. Set aside.

Stir eggs and milk in a large skillet until cooked completely. Season with salt and pepper or seasoned salt. Stir in cooked sausage and salsa.

Warm tortillas in microwave for 20 seconds or until warm and flexible. Place ⅔ cup egg mixture on tortilla; roll tortilla and place seam down on a lightly floured cookie sheet.

Freeze burritos for 1 hour, then place them in a large zip-top freezer bag and freeze.

To Serve

Remove burritos from zip-top bag. Microwave until heated through (about 2 minutes, turning burrito over after 1 minute). Or place frozen burritos on a foil-covered cookie sheet and bake at 350°F for 15 to 20 minutes or until defrosted.

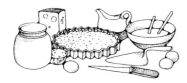

Breakfast Quiche

Yield: two 9-inch pies (8 servings each)

    1½ pounds ground pork sausage
        (can substitute cubed ham)
    2 tablespoons oregano
    1 large onion, diced
    2 nine-inch piecrusts, uncooked
    1 cup (4 ounces) shredded cheddar
        cheese

    8 large eggs
    1 cup milk
    salt and pepper

Preheat oven to 425°F. Place one prepared piecrust in each pie pan and pinch the edges of the crust using your thumb and fingers. Prick crusts all over with a fork and bake for 10 minutes. Remove crusts from the oven and let cool.

Meanwhile, in a large skillet, cook the sausage, diced onion, and oregano, breaking up the sausage. Cook until sausage is just browned, about 5 minutes. Drain and let cool, then divide mixture evenly in the 2 piecrusts.

In a medium bowl, beat together the eggs, milk, salt, and pepper. Divide the egg mixture evenly and pour it over the sausage mixture in each piecrust.

Cover the quiche and place in the freezer. When the quiche is frozen, remove it from the pie pan and wrap it in several layers of plastic wrap. Place the wrapped quiche in a large zip-top bag. Label "425°F, 30 minutes."

To Serve

Preheat oven to 425°F. Remove wrappings from the frozen quiche and place the pie pan on a baking sheet in the oven while it preheats. Bake for 30 minutes or until set and golden brown on top. Let quiche cool for 10 minutes before serving.

Sticky French Toast

Yield: 6 to 8 servings

⅔ cup brown sugar, firmly
   packed
½ cup (1 stick) butter or margarine,
   melted
2 teaspoons ground cinnamon
6 eggs, lightly beaten
1¾ cups milk
1 loaf (1 pound) French bread,
   cut into 1-inch slices
powdered sugar

Combine brown sugar, butter, and cinnamon. Spread evenly on a greased cookie sheet; set aside.

Combine eggs and milk in a shallow dish; place bread in dish and soak for 5 minutes, turning once. Place bread on sugar mixture.

Bake, uncovered, at 350°F for 25 to 30 minutes or until golden brown. Dust with powdered sugar in baking pan, then flip French toast over to serve brown sugar side up.

Cool half of toast and freeze in freezer bags for up to 2 months. To reheat, microwave on HIGH for 45 seconds or until hot.

Helpful Hint

Waffles can also be made in large batches and then frozen. I use a pancake mix to make waffles and I cook them in a Belgian waffle maker. The secret is to cook waffles on the lowest setting just until they hold their shape. Freeze the waffles, then place back in the waffle maker to thaw and heat. To reheat unfrozen waffles, microwave 20 seconds on HIGH, or place individual squares in the toaster on a very low setting until warm and crispy.

German Pancakes

Yield: two 9 x 13-inch pans (4 servings each)

12 eggs
2 cups milk
2 cups all-purpose flour
1 teaspoon salt
6 tablespoons melted butter
2 teaspoons cinnamon

Beat together eggs, milk, flour, and salt in a large bowl until smooth. Divide melted butter between pans, covering the bottom of each pan. Pour half of batter into each pan.

German pancakes are delicious topped with powdered sugar and maple syrup. For a more gourmet dish, top the pancake batter with bacon bits and sausage slices from your freezer. Or top the pancake batter with fresh apple slices (pre-frozen or fresh cut) sprinkled with cinnamon sugar.

Wrap each pan in plastic wrap, label "400°F, 25 minutes," and freeze.

To Serve

Preheat oven to 400°F. Discard plastic wrap and place pan in oven while it is preheating. Bake frozen for 30 minutes until golden brown on top and cooked through. Serve hot with maple syrup and powdered sugar sprinkled on top.

Cherry Crumble Coffee Cake

Yield: 8 to 10 servings

4 cups all-purpose flour
2 cups sugar
4 teaspoons baking powder
1 teaspoon salt
1 cup (2 sticks) butter
4 eggs
1 cup milk
2 cans cherry pie filling

Grease two 9 x 13-inch foil pans or two 9-inch deep-dish round or square pans.

To make the crumble topping, mix together the flour, sugar, baking powder, and salt. Soften the butter and, using a pastry cutter, cut it into the flour mixture until crumbly. Save 1 cup of this mixture for the topping.

Separate the eggs, placing the yolks in one bowl and the whites in another (make sure bowls are dry and clean). Set aside the bowl containing the egg whites.

Beat the egg yolks and then add the milk. Add the milk/egg-yolk mixture to the crumb mixture and stir with a wooden spoon until blended.

Beat the egg whites with clean beaters and a pinch of salt on high speed until the egg whites are stiff. Slowly fold the egg whites into the crumble batter.

Spread the batter evenly into prepared pans. Spread 1 can cherry pie filling over the batter in each pan. Then sprinkle the reserved crumble topping over each cake (1 cup topping per cake).

Bake one cake at 350°F for 45 minutes. Wrap the other cake in layers of plastic wrap, label "350°F, 45 minutes," and freeze.

Note: This crumble coffee cake can be made with any type of fruit pie filling.

To Serve
Remove wrappings from the frozen cake. Bake in preheated 350°F oven for 45 minutes. Serve warm.

Almond and Blueberry Granola
Yield: 16 cups granola

8 cups instant oats
3 cups whole almonds
½ cup brown sugar
1 teaspoon salt
1 teaspoon ground cinnamon
½ cup canola oil
½ cup honey
2 teaspoons vanilla extract
3 cups dried blueberries or other
    dried fruit

Preheat oven to 300°F. In a large bowl, mix oats, almonds, brown sugar, salt, and cinnamon.

In a small saucepan, warm the oil and honey. Whisk in the vanilla extract. Pour the honey, oil, and vanilla mixture over the oat mixture. Mix gently but well. Mix with spatula and then your hands.

Spread mixture on two cookie sheets and bake for 40 minutes, stirring after the first 20. Cool, then break up any clumps. Mix in dried fruits.

To Serve

Granola can be served in a bowl with cold milk, eaten as a dry snack, or mixed with fruit and yogurt.

Fruit and Granola Parfaits

Yield: 10 servings

4 to 5 cups granola
7 cups yogurt (any flavor)
fresh fruit (or frozen fruit, thawed)
10 plastic spoons
10 plastic cups (8 ounces each)

Set plastic cups in a shallow, square plastic container. In each cup, layer yogurt, then granola, then fruit. Place a spoon in each cup and set the square container in your refrigerator for a quick-and-easy breakfast.

Wheat-Berry Cereal

Yield: 8 to 10 servings

2 cups whole wheat
5 cups water
½ cup dried cranberries
½ cup brown sugar
½ cup whole flax (optional)

Place all ingredients in a slow cooker and cook on LOW overnight. In the morning, serve the cereal hot with sliced bananas or chopped trail mix.

Cool, label, and freeze the remaining cereal. Place 1- to 2-cup portions in sandwich-size zip-top bags for a quick breakfast.

To Serve

Remove the plastic bag and defrost the wheat-berry cereal in the microwave. Serve with sliced bananas or chopped fruit and nuts.

Drinks and Popsicles

White Grape Sparkle Punch

Yield: 8 servings

> 1 can (12 ounces) apple juice
>   concentrate, chilled
> 1 can (12 ounces) pink lemonade
>   concentrate, chilled
> 6 ounces (½ of 12-ounce can) white
>   grape juice concentrate, chilled
> 7½ cups water
> 2 cups club soda

In a large container, combine juice and lemonade concentrates; mix well. Stir in water and club soda. Serve immediately.

Strawberry Sparkle Punch

Yield: 6 servings

> 2 cups fresh strawberries
> 1½ cups cold water
> ½ cup lemon juice
> ½ cup sugar
> 1 cup Sprite, 7UP, or club soda

Blend strawberries, water, lemon juice, and sugar in a blender. Freeze berry mixture in a large zip-top bag.

To Serve

Defrost the berry mixture on the countertop or in the microwave. Then add the Sprite, 7UP, or club soda and more water to taste. Pour into glasses and garnish with fresh mint.

Helpful Hint

Mix leftover club soda with Kool-Aid and freeze in paper cups or a popsicle mold. Place in freezer until nearly frozen and then insert popsicle sticks. Kids love these popsicles, which contain less sugar than most store-bought popsicles.

Raspberry Lime Delight

Yield: 6 servings

> 1 can (12 ounces) limeade
>   concentrate, chilled
> 1 can (12 ounces) raspberry juice
>   concentrate, chilled
> 1½ one-liter bottles lemon-lime soda
> 1 lime, sliced, for garnish (optional)

In a one-gallon container with a tight lid, combine limeade and raspberry juice concentrates with water and lemon-lime soda. Freeze the mixture overnight.

To Serve

Thaw for 1 hour at room temperature or until the texture is like slush. Pour into a half-gallon pitcher and, if desired, garnish with fresh lime slices.

Cinnamon Apple Cider

Yield: 1 gallon cider

1 can (12 ounces) apple juice
    concentrate
3 cans water
3 cinnamon sticks
2 packages cherry-flavored beverage mix

Prepare the apple juice according to package directions. Place the apple juice and cinnamon sticks in a large saucepan. Bring to a boil, then reduce the heat to medium-low and simmer for 20 minutes. Add the beverage mix, and stir to dissolve. Serve hot.

Holiday Wassail

Yield: 2 batches of wassail (20 servings each)

5 cups sugar
8 cups hot water
4 cinnamon sticks
20 whole cloves
2 cans (12 ounces each) orange juice
    concentrate
2 cans (12 ounces each) lemonade
    concentrate
1 gallon apple juice
6 cups water

In a large pot, bring the hot water and sugar to a boil. Add the cinnamon sticks and cloves; lower heat and simmer for 1 hour. Let the mixture cool and remove the spices. Divide the mixture in half and freeze in large zip-top bags. Label "wassail mix" and freeze flat, stacking like bricks.

To Serve

Remove wrappings from one bag of wassail mix and heat in a large pot on the stovetop. Stir in 1 can orange juice concentrate, 1 can lemonade concentrate, and ½ gallon apple juice. Cook wassail until hot, stirring occasionally. Serve hot.

Berry Smoothies

Yield: 6 servings

2 cups yogurt (any flavor)
2 cups frozen fruit (berries, peaches,
bananas, etc.)
2 cups vanilla ice cream or berry sorbet
½ cup protein powder, any flavor
(optional)

Place all ingredients in a blender and blend until smooth. Freeze 2 cups of smoothie mixture in each of three sandwich-size zip-top bags. Label and store in the freezer.

To Serve

To make 2 servings, defrost smoothie mixture in microwave for 30 seconds on HIGH. Place frozen smoothie mixture in a blender. Add 1½ cups milk and 5 ice cubes, then blend.

Orange Julius

Yield: 6 servings

1 large can (16 ounces) orange juice (any
juice can be substituted)
1 cup powdered sugar
2 teaspoons vanilla
2 cups milk
1 cup water
24 ice cubes

Blend all ingredients in blender, then serve. Leftover juice can be used to make popsicles.

Orange Dreamsicles

Yield: seven 2½-ounce popsicles

6 ounces (½ of 12-ounce can) orange
juice concentrate
½ cup water
1 pint vanilla ice cream, softened (or
plain yogurt)

In a blender, mix all ingredients until smooth. Pour into popsicle molds, freeze for 1 hour, and insert sticks.

So that popsicle mold will be available for another batch, freeze popsicles until solid, remove them from the mold, and drop them into individual zip-top bags and freeze.

Fun Pops

Yield: 12 popsicles

3 cups punch or red juice (tropical punch, or red raspberry, cherry, or cranberry juice)

3 cups white punch or juice (lemonade, white grape juice, or coconut-flavored drink)

3 cups blue punch or juice (blue Kool-Aid or blue raspberry juice)

12 small (3-ounce) paper cups

12 popsicle sticks

Line up paper cups on a baking sheet. Pour 2 tablespoons of red punch or juice into each cup. Freeze for 2 to 3 hours or until firm-slushy. Remove from freezer and poke a popsicle stick into the center of each cup of punch or juice. Add 2 tablespoons of white punch or juice and freeze for 2 to 3 hours. Remove from freezer. Top with blue punch or juice and freeze until hard. Peel off paper cups to serve.

Fudge Pops

Yield: 20 popsicles

¼ cup (½ stick) butter, cubed

½ cup all-purpose flour

4 cups milk

1⅓ cups brown sugar, firmly packed

⅓ cup baking cocoa

1 teaspoon salt

2 teaspoons vanilla extract

20 popsicle molds or 3-ounce disposable plastic cups

popsicle sticks

In a large saucepan, melt butter over medium heat. Stir in flour until smooth; gradually add milk. Stir in the brown sugar, cocoa, and salt. Bring to a boil; cook and stir for 2 minutes or until thickened. Remove from heat; stir in vanilla. Cool for 20 minutes, stirring several times.

Pour ¼ cup liquid into each popsicle mold or plastic cup. Top each mold with a lid/stick, or insert a popsicle stick into each cup. Freeze until firm.

To Serve
Warm in microwave for 5 seconds, or under warm water until you can loosen the popsicle from the mold and serve.

Fruit and Yogurt Pops
Yield: 4 popsicles

    1 cup plain yogurt
    1 cup frozen or fresh fruit
    2 tablespoons honey
    4 wooden popsicle sticks or plastic
        spoons
    4 small (5-ounce) paper cups

Place yogurt, fruit, and honey in a blender and blend to desired consistency (chunky or smooth). Pour into paper cups, filling only ¾ full.

Cover cups with foil and make a slit in the center of the foil for the popsicle sticks. Insert the popsicle sticks or plastic spoons and freeze for at least 5 hours.

To Serve
Peel off the paper cups and enjoy.

Ice Cream Cakes

Grasshopper Ice Cream Cake

Yield: 10 servings

1 bag (32 ounces) cream-filled chocolate
    cookies
¼ cup (½ stick) butter, melted
4 cups mint chocolate-chip ice cream,
    softened
4 cups cookies-and-cream ice cream,
    softened
1½ cups hot-fudge ice cream topping

Reserve ⅓ of cookies. Crush rest of cookies in a zip-top bag or a food processor. Reserve ¼ cup crushed cookies for topping. Combine cookie crumbs and butter and press into the bottom of a 10-inch springform pan, two 9-inch pie pans, or a 9 x 13-inch pan. Freeze for 15 minutes.

Heat fudge topping in microwave on HIGH until pourable (15 to 20 seconds). Spread on top of the frozen cookie crust and place cookies around the sides of the pan, then freeze for 15 minutes.

Spread cookies-and-cream ice cream over fudge topping; freeze for 30 minutes. Spread mint chocolate-chip ice cream over vanilla layer; sprinkle with remaining ¼ cup cookie crumbs. Cover with plastic and freeze 1 hour or until firm. May be frozen for up to 2 months.

To Serve

Remove from the freezer 10 minutes before serving.

Snickers Ice Cream Cake

Yield: one 9 x 13-inch cake (10 servings)

2 cups powdered sugar
1 can (12 ounces) evaporated milk
⅔ cup chocolate chips
1 cup (2 sticks) butter, divided
1 teaspoon vanilla extract
3 cups chocolate wafer crumbs (about 48
    wafers)
½ gallon vanilla ice cream, softened
2 cups salted dry-roasted peanuts,
    crushed

In a large saucepan, bring the sugar, milk, chocolate chips, and ½ cup butter to a boil. Reduce heat and simmer, uncovered, for 8 minutes. Remove from the heat; stir in vanilla. Cool completely.

Melt the remaining ½ cup butter; toss with wafer crumbs. Press into the bottom of a 9 x 13-inch pan. Spread the softened ice cream over the crust and sprinkle with nuts. Freeze for 30 minutes.

Spread cooled sauce over nuts. Cover and freeze for 1 hour or until firm.

To Serve
Remove from the freezer 15 minutes before serving.

Coconut Almond Fudge Ice Cream Cake

Yield: one 10-inch round cake (10 servings)

1 package (13 ounces) macaroons, crushed
½ cup (1 stick) butter, melted
¾ cup hot-fudge ice cream topping
48 snack-size Mounds or Almond Joy candy bars
4 cups vanilla ice cream, softened
4 cups strawberry ice cream, softened (may substitute any other flavor but vanilla)
½ cup sliced almonds

Crush macaroons in a zip-top bag or food processor. Melt butter and combine with cookie crumbs. Press into the bottom of a 10-inch springform pan. Freeze for 15 minutes.

In microwave, heat fudge topping on HIGH until liquid (15 to 20 seconds). Spread over crust. Place candy bars around edge of pan. Freeze for 15 minutes. Remove vanilla ice cream from freezer to soften.

Spread vanilla ice cream (do not melt ice cream completely) over fudge topping; freeze for 30 minutes. Spread strawberry ice cream over vanilla layer; sprinkle with almonds. Cover with plastic wrap and freeze until firm.

To Serve
Remove from the freezer 10 minutes before serving. Remove sides of springform pan and slice the cake.

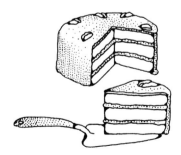

Jelly-Roll Ice Cream Cake

Yield: one cake (10 servings)

> 1 box chocolate cake mix
> ½ gallon ice cream (cherry chip is my
>   favorite)
> ½ cup powdered sugar

Mix cake mix according to box directions. Line a jelly-roll pan (large baking sheet with edges) with aluminum foil and spray with cooking spray. Spread cake batter in pan and bake at 350°F for 20 minutes or until light golden brown.

While baking the cake, spread two 24-inch sheets of aluminum foil on the counter, overlapping the sheets. Sprinkle foil with powdered sugar. Remove cake from the oven and flip it over onto the powdered sugar-covered foil sheets.

While cake is warm, cover it with softened ice cream. Roll up the cake, pulling the foil back as you roll. Then wrap the cake in more foil or plastic wrap and freeze.

To Serve

Remove cake from freezer 10 minutes before serving. Serve cake as is, or top with frosting or whipped cream. For a beautiful presentation, slice the cake across the swirls.

Triple-Layer Fudge Ice Cream Cake

Yield: 1 cake (12 servings)

> ½ cup hot-fudge ice cream topping
> 1 small container (8 ounces) whipped
>   topping
> 1 small package (4-serving-size)
>   chocolate instant pudding
> 1 cup cream-filled chocolate sandwich
>   cookies, chopped coarsely
> 12 vanilla ice cream sandwiches,
>   unwrapped

Pour fudge topping into medium bowl. Add 1 cup whipped topping; stir with wire whisk until blended. Add dry pudding mix; stir 2 minutes or until blended. Gently stir in chopped cream-filled cookies and set aside.

Line a baking sheet with a 24-inch piece of foil. Place 4 ice cream sandwiches side by side on the foil, then top with half of the whipped topping mixture. Repeat layers once.

Top with remaining 4 ice cream sandwiches. Frost top and sides of dessert with remaining whipped topping. Bring up foil sides. Double-fold top and ends to loosely seal packet.

Freeze packet on a baking sheet for at least 4 hours before serving.

To Serve
Remove from the freezer 10 minutes before serving.

Chocolate Devotion
Yield: one 10-inch round cake (10 servings)

25 unwrapped snack-sized chocolate candy bars
6 cookies-and-cream-flavor ice cream sandwiches
4 cups triple-chocolate fudge brownie ice cream, softened
1½ cups toffee pieces (see Homemade Toffee recipe on page 93)
1½ cups caramel topping
4 snack-sized candy bars, unwrapped

Place 5 ice cream sandwiches in the bottom of a 10-inch springform pan. Slice the last ice cream sandwich into triangles to fill in between the whole sandwiches.

Place snack-sized candy bars around the sides of the pan. Spread 2 cups triple-chocolate fudge brownie ice cream over the ice cream sandwiches. The ice cream will hold the candy bars in place. Freeze for 15 minutes.

Top the cake with toffee pieces and drizzle with caramel topping so the cake is completely covered. You can also top the cake with 10 dollops of caramel or whipped cream in a circle around the cake (one for each slice). Then slice 5 mini candy bars in half on a slant, and place a half in the middle of each dollop of caramel or whipped cream. Wrap cake in layers of plastic wrap and freeze for 1 hour or until firm. May be frozen for up to 2 months.

To Serve
Remove from the freezer 10 minutes before serving

Rainbow Sherbet Dessert
Yield: two 9-inch pies (about 6 servings each)

2 cups crushed vanilla wafers (about 60 cookies)
⅔ cup flaked coconut
⅔ cup chopped pecans
½ cup (1 stick) butter, melted
8 cups rainbow sherbet

Preheat oven to 350°F. In a large zip-top bag, combine cookie crumbs, coconut, pecans, and melted butter; press onto the bottom of two ungreased 9-inch cake pans or pie pans. Bake at 350°F for 10 to 12 minutes or until lightly browned. Cool for 10 minutes on a wire rack.

Scoop sherbet over the crust. Cover with layers of plastic wrap, then label and freeze.

To Serve
Remove from the freezer 10 minutes before serving.

Cookies

Soft & Chewy Gingersnaps

Yield: 3 dozen cookies

1½ cups shortening
2 cups sugar
2 eggs
½ cup honey
4½ cups all-purpose flour
4 teaspoons ground ginger
2 teaspoons baking soda
1½ teaspoons ground cinnamon
1 teaspoon ground cloves
¼ teaspoon salt

In a medium bowl, cream together the shortening and sugar. Add the eggs and then the honey. In a separate large bowl, stir together the dry ingredients. Add liquid ingredients to dry ingredients and blend well.

Place dough in a large zip-top bag and freeze.

To Serve

Preheat oven to 350°F. Remove frozen cookie dough from plastic bag and defrost in the microwave for 15 seconds on HIGH. Roll dough into balls and then roll each ball in coarse or granulated sugar. Bake at 350°F for 12 minutes, or until cookies are light brown and puffy.

This dough also makes delicious gingerbread cookies. Simply mix the dough as directed, then roll it out flat (½ inch thick) and use a gingerbread-man cookie cutter to cut the shapes. Bake cookies 1 inch apart on a greased baking pan at 350°F for 12 minutes. Cool and decorate cookies with frosting and candies.

Coconut Chocolate-Chip Cookies

Yield: 3 dozen cookies

2 cups (4 sticks) melted butter
2 cups sugar
2 cups brown sugar, firmly packed
4 eggs
2 teaspoons baking soda
2 teaspoons salt
3 cups all-purpose flour
8 cups oats
1 cup shredded coconut
1 cup chopped walnuts
1 cup semisweet chocolate chips

In a medium bowl, cream together the butter and sugar, then add the eggs. In a separate large bowl, mix together the flour, soda, salt, and flour, then add the butter mixture and blend until smooth.

Add the flour and oats. With a wooden spoon, stir in the coconut, nuts, and chocolate chips. Cut dough into 4 pieces and roll each into a log shape. Wrap each log in plastic wrap and then place in a large zip-top freezer bag. Label "325°F, 13 minutes," and freeze.

To Serve

Preheat oven to 325°F. Remove wrappings from the frozen cookie dough and place in the microwave for 10 seconds, just to soften the dough so you can break it apart with your fingers. For each cookie, place about 2 tablespoons of dough in your hand and roll it to form a ball. Place on greased baking sheet, then lightly press down on dough so that it forms a thick circle. Place cookies at least 2 inches apart. Bake at 325°F for 13 minutes. Cool cookies on a wire rack and enjoy.

Oatmeal Chocolate-Chip Cookies

Yield: 3 dozen cookies

¼ cup water
¾ cup shortening
1 cup brown sugar, firmly packed
1 egg
1 teaspoon vanilla

1 cup all-purpose flour
1 teaspoon salt
½ teaspoon baking soda
3 cups oats
½ cup semisweet or milk
  chocolate chips

Mix flour, salt, soda, and oats. In a separate bowl, cream together water, shortening, sugar, eggs, and vanilla. Add dry ingredients to shortening mixture and mix well. Stir in chocolate chips last.

Make 3 to 4 log-shaped rolls of dough and cover in plastic. Label "350°F, 13 minutes."

To Serve

For fresh-baked cookies, warm cookie dough in the microwave for 10 to 20 seconds or until dough breaks apart in your fingers. Drop by rounded tablespoonfuls on an ungreased cookie sheet and bake at 350°F for 13 minutes. Let cool on a wire rack.

Peanut Butter Oatmeal Cookies (Flourless)

Yield: about 6½ dozen cookies

    1½ cups peanut butter
    ½ cup (1 stick) butter, softened
    1 cup plus 2 tablespoons brown sugar,
        firmly packed
    1 cup sugar
    3 eggs
    2 teaspoons baking soda
    1 teaspoon vanilla extract
    ¾ teaspoon corn syrup
    4½ cups oats
    ¾ cup (6 ounces) miniature semisweet
        chocolate chips

In a large mixing bowl, cream the peanut butter, butter, and sugars. Add eggs, one at a time, beating well after each addition.

Beat in baking soda, vanilla, and corn syrup. Stir in oats, chips, and toffee bits. Dough will be sticky.

Drop by rounded tablespoonfuls 2 inches apart onto greased baking sheets. Bake at 350°F for 11 minutes or until lightly browned. (For best results, only bake 1 sheet at a time on the middle rack.) Cool cookies on baking sheet for 1 minute before transferring to wire racks.

Freeze cookies up to 3 months. You can also freeze extra cookie dough by rolling it into a log and wrapping it in plastic wrap. Label dough "350°F, 11 minutes" and freeze.

To Serve

Defrost in the microwave for 10 seconds on HIGH. Shape dough just as directed above, then bake and serve.

Big Fat Chewy Chocolate-Chip Cookies

Yield: 2 dozen cookies

    2½ cups all-purpose flour
    1 teaspoon salt
    1 teaspoon baking powder
    1 teaspoon baking soda
    3 cups oats
    1 cup (2 sticks) softened butter
    2 eggs
    2 teaspoon vanilla
    ½ cup sugar
    1½ cups brown sugar, firmly packed
    1½ cups semisweet chocolate chips

Preheat oven to 325°F. Line cookie sheets with parchment paper or spray with cooking spray. In a small bowl, mix together the flour, baking powder, soda, and salt. Then stir in the oats and set aside.

In a large bowl cream together the softened butter, sugars, eggs, and vanilla until creamy. Mix in the dry ingredients until well blended. Stir in the chocolate chips by hand.

Wrap half the cookie dough in layers of plastic in a log shape. Label "325°F, 15 minutes." Place in a zip-top bag and freeze up to 6 months.

Roll the remaining dough into golf ball-sized portions. Place on a cookie sheet and flatten until the cookies are ½ inch thick. Place cookies 3 inches apart, since they will spread. Bake 15 minutes or until just golden brown. Transfer to a wire rack. Serve warm or freeze for later.

To Serve

Defrost dough in the microwave for 20 to 30 seconds. (Just soften the dough—don't melt it.) Shape cookie dough into golf ball-size balls. Bake at 325°F for 15 minutes or until golden brown.

Soft Sugar Cookies
Yield: 1½ dozen cookies

1 cup sugar
3 cups all-purpose flour
½ teaspoon salt
1 teaspoon baking powder
½ teaspoon baking soda
½ cup sour cream
1 egg
1 teaspoon vanilla
1 cup shortening

Mix sugar and flour in a large bowl. Add salt and baking powder, then beat in shortening. When well blended, add sour cream and baking soda. Then add egg and vanilla.

Chill dough for at least 15 minutes and then roll out until ½ inch think. Cut using a 2½-inch round cookie cutter. Bake cookies on a greased cookie sheet at 350°F for 11 to 12 minutes, then cool on a wire rack.

Once cookies have cooled, they can be frozen as long as they are not frosted (frosting does not freeze well). Alternately, you may freeze half the cookie dough. Roll the dough into a log shape, wrap it in plastic, label it "350°F, 11 to 12 minutes," and freeze.

To Serve

Defrost pre-baked cookies on the counter for 10 minutes. Defrost frozen cookie dough in the microwave for 10 to 15 seconds, being careful not to melt the dough, and bake as directed. Frost cookies with Creamy Frosting (see page 97) and serve.

Chocolate Caramel Cookies

Yield: 2 dozen cookies

> 1 devil's food cake mix
> 2 eggs
> ⅓ cup vegetable or canola oil
> 24 Rollos candies, unwrapped

Thoroughly combine ingredients with a wooden spoon. Then place 2 tablespoons cookie dough in your hand and flatten it. Place a Rollo in the center and wrap the cookie dough around it to form a ball. Place on an ungreased cookie sheet and bake at 350°F for 7 to 10 minutes. Sprinkle cookies with powdered sugar and serve warm.

To Freeze

Place cookie-dough balls (with Rollo wrapped inside) on a cookie sheet for 1 hour. Then put frozen dough balls in a large zip-top bag and freeze for up to 3 months.

To Serve

Remove frozen cookie-dough balls from freezer and place on a cookie sheet for 10 minutes. Then bake at 350°F for 7 to 10 minutes and serve. Baked cookies may be frozen for up to 3 months.

No-Bake Cookies

Yield: 4 dozen cookies

> 2 cups sugar (I use 1¼ cups sugar and ½ cup clover honey)
> ½ cup (1 stick) butter
> ½ cup milk
> ⅓ cup unsweetened cocoa powder
> ⅓ cup chocolate protein powder (optional)
> 1 tablespoon ground flax (optional)
> ⅔ cup chunky peanut butter
> 3 cups oats
> 2 teaspoons vanilla extract

Place wax paper or aluminum foil on 2 cookie sheets. In a medium saucepan, combine sugar, butter, milk, and cocoa. Cook over medium heat, stirring constantly, until mixture come to a rolling boil.

Remove pan from heat; cool 1 minute. Add peanut butter and stir to blend. Add oats and vanilla; mix well.

Quickly drop mixture by heaping teaspoonfuls onto the wax paper or foil. Cool completely in the freezer, or in the fridge if your freezer is full. Place chilled cookies in large zip-top plastic bags and store in the freezer up to 2 months.

To Serve
Let frozen cookies defrost on the countertop at room temperature for a few minutes. Serve cookies cold.

White Chocolate-Chip Macadamia-Nut Cookies

Yield: 2 dozen cookies

½ cup (1 stick) butter
½ cup sugar
½ cup brown sugar, firmly packed
1 egg
1 teaspoon vanilla
1¼ cups all-purpose flour
½ teaspoon soda
¼ teaspoon salt
¾ cup oats

1 bag (12 ounces) HERSHEY'S white chocolate-chip macadamia-nut mix (or purchase nuts and chips separately)

Preheat oven to 350°F. Mix flour, sugars, salt, and soda. In a separate bowl, cream butter, egg, and vanilla. Add flour mixture to butter mixture, mixing thoroughly. Stir in oats, then the white chocolate-chip mixture. (Batter should be stiff.)

Roll dough into three logs and wrap each in plastic wrap, then place in freezer. Or bake cookies and freeze them in a large zip-top bag.

To Serve
Warm cookie dough in microwave for 10 to 20 seconds or just until you can pull the dough apart with your fingers. Drop by spoonfuls onto an ungreased cookie sheet. Bake at 350°F for 10 to 12 minutes or until cookies are golden brown. Cool for 3 minutes on cookie sheet, then place cookies on wire racks to finish cooling.

Oatmeal Pumpkin Cookies

Yield: 4 dozen cookies

4 cups all-purpose flour
3 cups oats
2 teaspoons baking soda
2 teaspoons ground cinnamon
1 teaspoon salt
2 cups (4 sticks) butter
2 cups brown sugar, firmly packed
2 cups sugar
2 eggs
2 teaspoons vanilla
2 cups packed pumpkin
1 cup semisweet chocolate chips

Combine flour, oats, baking soda, cinnamon, and salt in a large bowl. In a separate bowl, cream butter and sugars. Blend in eggs and vanilla and mix well, then stir in pumpkin. Combine flour mixture with butter mixture, then add chocolate chips. Roll half the dough into logs and wrap in plastic wrap. Place dough in large zip-top bags and label "350°F, 20 minutes."

Chill the remaining dough for 30 minutes so that cookies will be more plump. Drop dough by heaping tablespoonfuls onto cookie sheet. Bake at 350°F for 20 to 23 minutes.

To Serve

Defrost cookie dough just until you can break it apart with your fingers. Drop dough by heaping tablespoonfuls onto cookie sheet. Bake at 350°F for 20 minutes.

Fudge Cookie Bars

Yield: 1 cookie sheet of bars (about 20)

1 cup (2 sticks) butter, softened
2 cups brown sugar, firmly packed
1 teaspoon baking soda
2 eggs
2 teaspoons vanilla
2½ cups all-purpose flour
3 cups oats
1½ cups semisweet chocolate chips
1 can (14 ounce) sweetened condensed
    milk
2 teaspoons vanilla

Set aside 2 tablespoons butter. In a large bowl, beat the remaining butter for 30 seconds, then mix in brown sugar and baking soda. Add eggs and vanilla. Beat in the remaining flour and oats.

In a medium saucepan, combine the chocolate chips, sweetened condensed milk, and 2 tablespoons reserved butter. Stir over low heat until chocolate melts. Remove from heat. Stir in vanilla.

Press ⅔ of the oat mixture into the bottom of a cookie sheet. Spread filling evenly over the oat mixture. Use your fingers to make flat pieces of the leftover oat mixture, and place them on top of the filling.

Bake at 350°F for about 20 minutes or until top is lightly browned. Cool in pan on a wire rack and then cut into bars. Individually wrap bars and store in an airtight container in the freezer for up to 4 months.

To Serve
Remove bars from freezer and thaw. Serve cold.

Pudding-Mix Cookies
Yield: 3 dozen cookies

    2 cups (4 sticks) butter
    1½ cups brown sugar, firmly packed
    ½ cup sugar
    1 large package (5 ounces) instant vanilla
        pudding mix
    4 eggs
    2 teaspoons vanilla
    5 cups all-purpose flour
    2 teaspoons baking soda
    4 cups semisweet chocolate chips
    2 cups chopped walnuts or M&M's
        (optional)

Preheat oven to 350°F. Cream together the butter and sugars, then beat in the pudding mix. Stir in the eggs and vanilla. Mix together the flour and soda and then blend into the wet ingredients.

Stir in the chocolate chips and the walnuts or M&M's. Roll half the dough into logs and wrap in plastic wrap. Place dough in a large zip-top bag and label "350°F, 12 minutes."

Drop the remaining dough by spoonfuls onto greased cookie sheets and bake at 350°F for 12 minutes. Place on a wire rack to cool and then serve.

To Serve
Warm cookie dough in the microwave for 10 to 20 seconds or until you can break it apart with your fingers. Drop by spoonfuls on a ungreased cookie sheet and bake at 350°F for 12 minutes. Let cookies cool on a wire rack and serve.

Desserts

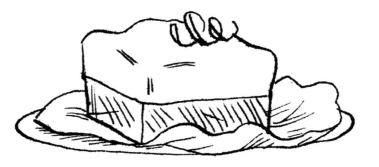

Chocolate-Apple Snack Cake

Yield: two 9 x 13-inch cakes (12 servings each)

3 cups all-purpose flour
½ cup baking cocoa
2 teaspoons baking soda
1 teaspoon salt
2 cups water
½ cup vegetable oil or applesauce
2 teaspoons lemon juice
2 teaspoons vanilla extract
2 cups puréed or diced baking apples
    (peeled)
1½ cups sugar
½ teaspoon ground cinnamon

In a medium bowl, combine flour, cocoa, baking soda, and salt.

Combine water, oil, lemon juice, and vanilla; add to dry ingredients and stir just until combined. For a moist chocolate cake, purée the apples (or use applesauce), or for more texture in the cake, chop the apples, toss them with sugar and cinnamon, and fold them into the batter.

Pour into two greased 9 x 13-inch baking pans. Bake at 350°F for 30 to 35 minutes or until toothpick inserted in center of cake comes out clean. Cut into squares and freeze half for later. Serve the rest warm.

To Serve
Remove cake from freezer and thaw on countertop.

Chocolate Snack Cake

Yield: two 9 x 13-inch cakes (12 servings each)

3⅓ cups all-purpose flour
4 cups brown sugar, firmly packed
1 cup cocoa powder
4 teaspoons baking powder
4 teaspoons baking soda
4 teaspoons vanilla
2 teaspoons salt
4 cups water
1⅓ cups canola or vegetable oil (or
    applesauce)
2 cups chocolate chips

Mix dry ingredients in a large bowl. Stir in the vanilla, salt, water, and oil or applesauce.

Add chocolate chips, then spread batter in two 9 x 13-inch pans. Bake at 350°F for 40 to 45 minutes

This cake does not need frosting, but to make it look festive, drizzle caramel or melted white chocolate over the top. For Christmas, sprinkle crushed candy canes on top with drizzled white chocolate.

Cherry Chocolate Cupcakes

Yield: 2½ dozen cupcakes

Chocolate Cream-Cheese Filling
    1 package (8 ounces) cream cheese, softened
    ⅓ cup sugar
    1 large egg
    ⅛ teaspoon salt
    1 cup semisweet chocolate chips

Chocolate Cupcakes
    1 chocolate cake mix
    3 eggs
    1¼ cups water

    ⅓ cup applesauce (substitute for oil)
    1 container (16 ounces) white butter-cream frosting
    1 can cherry pie filling

Directions for Chocolate Cream-Cheese Filling
Beat cream cheese, sugar, egg, and salt in small bowl until smooth and creamy. Stir in chocolate chips.

Directions for Cupcakes
Heat oven to 350°F. Line medium muffin pans with paper baking cups and set aside.

In a large bowl, mix together cake mix, water, eggs, and applesauce. Fill muffin cups ⅔ full with batter. Spoon 1 tablespoon of chocolate cream-cheese filling into center of each cupcake.

Bake at 350°F for 25 to 30 minutes or until toothpick inserted in cake portion comes out clean. Remove from pan and transfer to wire rack. Cool completely.

Freeze cupcakes in a large zip-top bag. To serve, remove cupcakes from freezer and defrost on countertop, or microwave for 30 seconds.

Using a #5 tip and a pastry bag (if using a zip-top bag, cut a small hole in one corner of the bag), pipe a line around the outer edge of each cupcake. Place cherry pie filling on top of the cupcake to the outer edge of the frosting. To finish, pipe frosting in lines across the top of each cupcake so it resembles a cherry pie.

Toffee Crunch Cake

Yield: two 8-inch square cakes (9 servings each)

    1 chocolate cake mix
    1 small cup semisweet chocolate
        chips
    1 can (14 ounces) sweetened
        condensed milk
    1½ cups (12 ounces) caramel topping
    1 medium container (12 ounces)
        frozen whipped topping
    3 chocolate toffee bars, broken into
        small chunks

Preheat oven to 350°F. Prepare cake mix according to package directions; divide between 2 prepared 8-inch square foil pans. After 10 minutes of baking, sprinkle with chocolate chips. Continue baking until cakes are done.

Remove cakes from the oven. While they are still hot, poke holes in the top with the end of a wooden spoon. Pour half of the sweetened condensed milk over one cake, then half over the other. When cakes have cooled, wrap them in layers of plastic wrap and freeze.

To Serve

Thaw whipped topping. Remove cakes from freezer 30 minutes before serving time. Pour caramel topping over the cakes, then spread whipped topping on the cakes and top with small pieces of chocolate toffee bar. Serve chilled.

Peanut Butter Fingers (No-Bake)

Yield: 20 bars

    1½ cups graham-cracker crumbs
    3½ cups powdered sugar
    1½ cups peanut butter
    1 cup (2 sticks) butter, melted
    1 bag (12 ounces) milk chocolate chips

In a glass bowl, melt chocolate chips in oven on lowest setting (170°F). This should take about 5 minutes. Combine graham-cracker crumbs with powdered sugar and peanut butter and mix well. Blend in melted butter. Press the mixture in a 9 x 13-inch pan. Spread melted chocolate chips over the peanut butter mixture. Chill until just set (1 to 2 hours) and cut into bars.

Wrap bars individually and freeze up to 3 months. Another option is to freeze bars for 1 hour on a cookie sheet, and then transfer them to a large zip-top bag and place in freezer.

To Serve

Let bars defrost for 10 minutes on the counter. Serve with large glasses of cold milk.

Mint Brownies

Yield: 9 x 13-inch pan (16 servings)

1 cup (2 sticks) margarine
½ cup cocoa powder
2 tablespoons honey
4 eggs
2 cups sugar
1¾ cups all-purpose flour
½ tablespoon baking powder
½ teaspoon salt
1 cup chopped walnuts
1½ cups (12 ounces) chocolate frosting

Mint Frosting
5 tablespoons margarine
dash salt
1 tablespoon light corn syrup
2⅓ cups powdered sugar
½ teaspoon mint extract
1 to 2 drops green food coloring
3 tablespoons milk

Melt margarine and mix in cocoa powder. Allow to cool. Add honey, eggs, sugar, flour, baking powder, and salt. Mix well. Add nuts. Pour batter into a greased 9 x 13-inch baking pan. Bake at 350°F for 25 minutes. Cool in pan on a wire rack.

To make the mint frosting, soften the margarine, and add the salt, corn syrup, and powdered sugar. Beat until smooth and fluffy. Mix in the mint extract and green food coloring. Add milk gradually until the consistency is a little thinner than cake frosting.

Spread mint frosting over the brownies. Do not slice the brownies. Wrap them in plastic and place them in the freezer.

To Serve

Remove brownies from the freezer and carefully add a layer of chocolate frosting. Slice and serve.

Buttery Piecrust

Yield: 4 single-layer piecrusts

5⅓ cups all-purpose flour
¼ cup sugar
1 teaspoon salt
¾ cup shortening
1⅓ cups (2 sticks plus 5 tablespoons)
    butter, cubed
1 cup ice water

In a food processor, mix together the flour, salt, and sugar. Add the shortening and butter and pulse the processor with 15 on/off pulses. The mixture should be dry and flaky. Add the ice-cold water a few tablespoons at a time, with 5 rapid on/off pulses each time. Stop and feel the dough; it should be just moist enough that it can clump together. If necessary, add more water by teaspoonfuls, with 2 to 3 pulses after each addition. The total mixing time should be less than 2 minutes, and the dough should not form a ball; it should remain flaky.

With floured hands, remove the dough from the food processor and divide it into 4 disks. Place each disk in a large zip-top freezer bag, label it "400°F, 15 minutes," and freeze.

To Serve

Remove one pie-dough disk from the freezer and let it sit on the counter until thawed (about 45 minutes). Roll dough out, using a sheet of plastic wrap on top and bottom to keep it from sticking to the counter or roller. Place the dough in a 9-inch pie pan. Pinch the dough around the edges using your thumb and two fingers (from the other hand) to give it a finished look.

If your recipe calls for a pre-baked crust, preheat the oven to 400°F and prick the dough all over with a fork. Line the crust with foil and place a cup of dry rice or beans (or use pie weights) on the foil to weigh it down.

Bake for 15 minutes. Remove crust from the oven, cool for a few minutes, and carefully remove the foil and rice, beans, or weights. Reduce the heat to 350°F and cook for an additional 10 minutes, until the crust is golden. Cool completely before filling.

This piecrust can be used for fruit pies, quiche, custards, or chicken pot pies.

Peach Pie

Yield: two 9-inch pies (8 servings each)

  6 cups peeled, sliced peaches
  1½ cups sugar
  2 tablespoons minute tapioca
  ¼ teaspoon nutmeg
  ¼ teaspoon cinnamon

Place sliced peaches in a bowl with sugar, tapioca, and nutmeg. Toss until peaches are evenly coated and sugar is mostly dissolved.

Line 2 pie pans with heavy foil, placing a piece of plastic wrap over foil. Put 3 cups filling in each pan. Loosely fold plastic wrap around filling and freeze until firm. When filling is frozen solid, remove from pans and wrap tightly in more plastic. Label "375°F, 45 minutes" and return to freezer until ready to use.

To Serve

Preheat oven to 375°F. Take pie filling out of the freezer and remove the wrappings. Place the frozen filling in a pie pan lined with an unbaked piecrust. Top filling with ¼ cup (½ stick) diced butter, then sprinkle with cinnamon. Top pie with an additional piecrust (cut several slits in the top crust to vent steam), seal well, and bake for 45 to 50 minutes at 375°F.

Caramel Apple Crisp

Yield: two 9 x 13-inch pan (10 servings each)

  16 cups peeled, sliced apples (Granny
      Smith or Golden Delicious)
  1½ cups sugar
  2 tablespoons cinnamon
  ½ cup (2 sticks) margarine, melted
  2 cups all-purpose flour
  2 cups oats

2 cups brown sugar, firmly packed
½ teaspoon soda
½ teaspoon baking powder
½ teaspoon salt
1 cup (1 stick) margarine
1 bottle (10 ounces) caramel sauce
  (optional)

Stir cinnamon sugar and ½ cup melted margarine into apples. Place apple mixture in a buttered 9 x 13-inch pan. (For easy cleanup, use an aluminum baking pan, or a foil-lined glass baking pan.) Mix remaining ingredients with a pastry blender or two forks. Sprinkle over apples in pans.

Wrap one pan in several layers of plastic wrap and label "350°F, 45 minutes." Place other pan in 350°F oven for 45 minutes. Serve hot with vanilla and caramel ice cream. Pour caramel sauce on top.

To Serve
Defrost in refrigerator or on countertop, then bake at 350°F for 45 minutes. If frozen, bake for 1 hour.

Fruit Pizza
Yield: 12-inch pizza (10 servings)

  1 package (16 ounces) frozen sugar
    cookie dough
  1 package (8 ounces) reduced-fat cream
    cheese
  ⅓ cup sugar
  1 teaspoon vanilla extract
  1 firm banana, peeled, and sliced
  1 large can (29 ounces) sliced peaches
  2 kiwi fruit, peeled and sliced
  ½ to 1 cup sliced strawberries
  ½ cup sliced cherries (if available)
  ½ cup frozen blueberries
  2 to 4 tablespoons chocolate syrup or
    melted semisweet chocolate

Defrost sugar cookie dough on countertop, or remove plastic wrap and defrost in the microwave for 20 to 30 seconds or until you can shape it with your hands.

Place cookie dough on a greased 12-inch pizza pan, pressing the dough down with your fingertips until it evenly covers the bottom of the pan. Bake at 350°F for 10 to 12 minutes or until light brown and puffy.

Cool completely in pan on wire rack. Drain sliced peaches, reserving 1 tablespoon juice. In a small mixing bowl, beat cream cheese, sugar, reserved 1 tablespoon of peach juice, and vanilla until smooth. Spread over cooled cookie crust.

Just before you are ready to serve the fruit pizza, arrange peach slices in a circle along the outside of the pizza over the cream cheese. Arrange bananas next, then follow with the strawberries, kiwis, and cherries. Save the blueberries for the center of the fruit pizza.

Drizzle chocolate syrup over the fruit and sprinkle a little powdered sugar on top. Slice like a pizza and serve chilled.

Cinnamon Twists

Yield: 20 twists

    4 tablespoons yeast
    4 cups warm milk
    1 cup sugar
    4 teaspoons salt
    1 cup shortening
    4 eggs
    12 cups all-purpose flour

Glaze

    4 ounces cream cheese (½ package), at
        room temperature
    1 cup powdered sugar
    ¼ cup (½ stick) unsalted butter, at room
        temperature
    ½ teaspoon vanilla extract

Cinnamon Sugar

    2 tablespoons cinnamon
    2 cups brown sugar, firmly packed

Warm milk in the microwave for 1 to 2 minutes. Mix together all remaining ingredients except 6 cups flour. Then stir in remaining flour and add a little more if the dough sticks to your fingers. (The dough will be different depending on the humidity.)

Place dough in a large greased bowl in a warm oven to rise for 25 minutes. (I set my oven to 170°F and then turn it off when I am ready to put the dough in.) When dough has doubled in size, remove it from the oven and punch it down. On a lightly floured countertop, roll dough into a long rectangle. Spread the dough with softened margarine and then top with cinnamon sugar.

With a pizza cutter, slice dough into 24 one-inch strips. Roll a piece of dough into a snake shape, then drape the middle of the "snake" over your forefinger and twist the two sides together. Place twist on greased baking sheet, and repeat with remaining pieces of dough. Place twists at least ½ inch apart on baking sheets.

Place baking sheets in the freezer for 1 hour. After twists are frozen, place them in large zip-top bags. Label and freeze.

To Serve

Remove cinnamon twists from the freezer and let them rise all night on a greased baking sheet with greased plastic on top. Or let breadsticks rise in a warm oven until they are doubled in size.

Preheat oven to 425°F. Bake twists for 15 to 20 minutes or until golden brown. Remove from the pan and cool on a wire rack. When breadsticks are cool, make the glaze by combining the cream cheese, powdered sugar, butter, and vanilla in a medium bowl. With an electric mixer, beat until smooth. Using a zip-top bag with a hole in one bottom corner, cover the twists with glaze. Serve warm.

Chocolate-Dipped Cream Puffs

Yield: 30 cream puffs

1¼ cups water
⅔ cup (1 stick plus 3 tablespoons) butter
1¼ cups all-purpose flour
¼ teaspoon salt
5 eggs
1 small container (8 ounces) whipped topping
1 cup semisweet chocolate chips
1 tablespoon butter
½ tablespoon milk

In a large saucepan, bring water and butter to a boil over medium heat. Add flour and salt; stir until a smooth ball forms. Remove saucepan from the heat; let stand for 5 minutes. Add the eggs, one at a time, beating well after each addition. Continue stirring until mixture is smooth and shiny.

Roll dough into 1½-inch balls. Place 2 inches apart on greased baking sheets. Bake at 400°F for 30 to 35 minutes or until golden brown. Cool the puffs on the baking sheets.

To fill the cream puffs, use a plastic squeeze bottle with a narrow tip to poke a hole in the top on the cream puff and squeeze in the whipped topping. You can also use a #7 round tip with a pastry bag or a resealable plastic bag.

Once cream puffs have been filled, place chocolate chips, 1 tablespoon butter, and ½ tablespoon milk in a microwave-safe glass bowl. Heat in microwave on HIGH for 1 minute, stirring chocolate every 10 seconds until it is smooth and melted. Add more milk until chocolate is smooth and creamy.

Dip top of each cream puff in the chocolate and sprinkle with powdered sugar or candy sprinkles. Set cream puffs on a lightly greased cookie sheet in the freezer for 1 hour. After they are frozen, drop them into large zip-top bags and freeze.

To Serve

Remove cream puffs from the freezer and allow to defrost for 10 minutes.

JELL-O Parfaits

Yield: 6 servings

2 packages (3 ounces each) strawberry-
    flavored JELL-O gelatin
3 cups frozen pound cake, cut into
    1-inch cubes
2¼ cups frozen whipped topping
2 tablespoons sugar
⅛ teaspoon ground cinnamon
6 strawberries, washed and hulled

Cook strawberry JELL-O according to package directions. Pour into a 9 x 13-inch pan. Refrigerate until set. Gelatin does not freeze well, so this part must be done on the day you will serve the dish or the night before. Set the frozen, cubed pound cake and the whipped topping on the counter to defrost while gelatin is setting.

When gelatin has set, slice into 1-inch cubes. In each of six 1½-cup parfait glasses or dessert dishes, layer ¼ cup cake cubes, ⅓ cup cubed gelatin, 3 tablespoons whipped topping. Repeat.

Combine sugar and cinnamon; sprinkle over whipped topping. Top with a strawberry.

Butterscotch Pecan Fudge

Yield: 9 x 13-inch pan (30 servings)

    1 tablespoon butter, softened
    4 cups (two 12-ounce bags) semisweet
        chocolate chips
    2 cans (14 ounces each) sweetened
        condensed milk
    4 teaspoons vanilla extract
    ½ cup caramel topping
    1½ cups butterscotch chips
    1 cup pecan pieces

Line a 9 x 13-inch pan with foil; grease foil with butter and set pan aside.

In a heavy saucepan, melt chocolate chips in sweetened condensed milk over low heat, stirring until smooth. Remove from heat. Add vanilla; stir for 3 to 4 minutes or until creamy. Spread mixture in prepared pan. Refrigerate for 10 minutes or until firm.

Drizzle a layer of caramel over the chilled fudge. Place in the freezer for 15 minutes or until caramel is firm. With a knife, divide fudge in half. Stack one layer of fudge on top of the other and then top with pecan pieces and butterscotch chips. Wrap in layers of plastic wrap and freeze.

To serve
Remove fudge from freezer and place on countertop for 30 minutes. Slice fudge into 1-inch squares. Serve cold.

Homemade Toffee

Yield: 2 pounds toffee

    1 pound (4 sticks) butter
    ⅔ cup water
    2 cups sugar
    1 to 2 large HERSHEY'S Symphony
        chocolate bars

Butter a cookie sheet and set it aside. In a large pot on the stove, combine butter and water. Set burner at highest temperature. Add sugar to the pan and stir constantly with a wooden spoon until mixture comes to a boil. Continue stirring until the mixture turns golden brown—the color of a paper bag. This will take around 30 minutes. If the mixture does not get dark enough, it will not harden, but will turn into a soft caramel.

Pour toffee on the cookie sheet. While the toffee is still warm, break the chocolate bars into pieces and place the pieces on the toffee. Once the chocolate melts, spread it evenly on the toffee.

Let the toffee harden completely at room temperature. Then break it into chunks and store in zip-top freezer bags for up to 12 months.

To Serve

Let toffee come to room temperature by letting it cool on the counter or in the refrigerator in an airtight container. Toffee tastes best when served cold.

Soft Caramel Corn

Yield: 30 servings

3 packages (3.5 ounces each) plain microwave popcorn, popped
2¼ cups brown sugar, firmly packed
1 cup corn syrup
1 cup butter
1 can (14 ounces) sweetened condensed milk (reserve until the end)

Pop the popcorn and then place it in a large bowl. Shake and toss the bowl so that the unpopped kernels sink to the bottom. Discard unpopped kernels.

In a saucepan over medium-high heat, cook the brown sugar, corn syrup, and butter, stirring constantly. Heat to 270°F or until a small amount dropped into cold water turns into a hardened thread. Remove the mixture from the heat and carefully pour in the can of sweetened condensed milk. Stir until smooth.

While stirring the popcorn, pour a small amount of caramel at a time over the popcorn. Repeat until all the popcorn is covered with caramel. Cool at least 10 minutes before serving. Reserve leftover caramel corn in zip-top bags in the freezer.

To Serve

Remove caramel corn from the freezer 10 minutes before serving.

White Chocolate Popcorn

Yield: 6 to 8 servings

   1 package (12 ounces) white chocolate
        chips (I use Guittard brand)
   ¾ cup unpopped white popcorn kernels
   1 package Peanut M&M's (or any other
        small chocolate candies)
   3 tablespoons canola oil

Pour canola oil and unpopped popcorn into a large pot over medium-high heat. Lightly stir until all popcorn kernels are covered in oil, and then place the lid on pot. When kernels start to pop, lift lid carefully and stir occasionally with a wooden spoon until all kernels have popped. Turn off heat and pour popcorn into a large bowl to cool.

Place white chocolate chips in a microwave-safe bowl and heat on HIGH for 1 minute, stirring every 10 seconds until chocolate has melted.

Pour melted chocolate over popped popcorn in a large mixing bowl, tossing gently. Add candy pieces and stir. Place popcorn in large zip-top bags and freeze.

To Serve

Remove a bag of popcorn from the freezer, open it, and let it sit on the countertop to defrost.

Sticky Trail Mix

Yield: 10 servings

   1 cup corn syrup
   1 cup sugar
   ¾ cup (1½ sticks) butter
   6 ounces (½ of 12-ounce box) Rice Chex
        cereal
   6 ounces (½ of 12-ounce box) Crispex
        cereal

3½ cups mini pretzels
½ cup sliced almonds
½ cup shredded coconut
1 cup M&M's

Preheat oven to 350°F. Place almonds on a foil-covered baking sheet in the oven for 6 minutes. In a large bowl, combine cereal, almonds, and coconut.

In a medium saucepan, melt butter. Add corn syrup and sugar and mix thoroughly. Boil mixture for 2 minutes.

Pour over cereal mixture and mix well. Add M&M's and stir until combined. Spread trail mix onto two large baking sheets or a large sheet of wax paper to cool. Place in zip-top bags and serve right away or store in the freezer for later.

To Serve
Pull zip-top bag out of the freezer and open the bag. Let the trail mix set on the counter to defrost. Do not microwave.

CoolWhip Cake Frosting
Yield: Frosting for one 9-inch round cake

1 large container (16 ounces)
    CoolWhip brand whipped
    topping
1 package (8 ounces) cream
    cheese, softened
2 tablespoons milk
1 cup powdered sugar
1 teaspoon vanilla

Place all ingredients in a large bowl and whip until smooth. Add food coloring if desired.

Before frosting a cake, freeze the cake for at least 1 hour. It will be much easier to frost.

You can make this frosting up to 3 days in advance and store it in the refrigerator. Do not freeze the frosting, because it tends to separate and crystallize.

For detailing, place a small amount of frosting in a sandwich-size zip-top plastic bag. Then cut off a small piece of one bottom corner of the bag. Squeeze the bag and decorate the cake as you would using a pastry bag.

Creamy Frosting

Yield: 2 cups frosting

> ½ cup (1 stick) butter
> 1½ cups powdered sugar
> ¼ teaspoon vanilla

Cream together butter, powdered sugar, and vanilla. Add food coloring for seasonal cookies. Frostings do not freeze well, but this one will keep for about a month in an airtight container in the refrigerator.

Helpful Hint

Decorate brownies for Valentines' Day. Use a heart-shaped cookie cutter to cut out the center of each brownie. Then fill each heart-shaped space with white frosting. Lightly dust a cookie sheet with cocoa powder, then place brownies on sheet for 20 minutes, before serving so that frosting can set up.

Main Dishes

Poultry

Chicken Marengo
Yield: 8 servings

5 boneless, skinless chicken breast halves
1 packet spaghetti sauce mix (or beef stew mix)
2 tablespoons olive oil
1 cup dried onions (or 2 medium onions, diced)
1 garlic clove, minced
1 cup water
2 teaspoons (2 cubes) beef bouillon
1 can (14½ ounces) diced tomatoes
1 bay leaf
½ pound mushrooms, chopped (optional)
4 to 5 cups cooked rice

Trim fat off chicken breasts, then cut chicken into 1-inch cubes. Place cubed chicken in a bowl and sprinkle the packet of spaghetti sauce mix onto the chicken, stirring until the chicken is covered with the mix.

Heat oil in a large nonstick skillet over medium heat. Add chicken and quickly brown on all sides. Do not overcook chicken or it will be dry.

Add onions and garlic and cook until onions are slightly browned. Add water, beef bouillon, and bay leaf and bring to a boil. Reduce heat, cover, and simmer for 30 minutes or until chicken is tender and no longer pink.

Place cooked rice on a serving dish. Remove chicken from heat and place half on top of the rice. Place the remaining chicken in a bowl and cool in the fridge.

Add mushrooms to skillet with 1 tablespoon margarine. Cover and cook over low heat for 15 minutes. Do not stir; wait until mushrooms are brown and crisp on the bottom, then flip and brown the other side. Pour mushroom mixture over chicken and sprinkle with parsley to garnish.

When the other half of the chicken marengo is cool, place it in a large zip-top bag, label it "chicken marengo, warm and serve on rice," and freeze.

To Serve
Defrost chicken marengo in the refrigerator overnight or in the microwave for 4 minutes or until warmed through. Serve over warmed-up cooked rice.

Chicken Pot Pie

Yield: two 9-inch pot pies (6 to 8 servings each)

4 cups cubed chicken (or ham, turkey, or
    beef)
4 medium potatoes, peeled and diced
2 cups sliced carrots
1 medium onion, chopped
1 cup (2 sticks) butter or margarine
1 cup all-purpose flour
1 tablespoon salt
1 teaspoon dried thyme
1 teaspoon pepper
3 cups chicken broth
1½ cups milk
1 cup frozen peas
1 cup frozen corn
pastry for two double-crust 9-inch pies, or
    use biscuit/baking mix to make crust

Reduce heat, cover, and simmer vegetables for 8 to 10 minutes. Boil potatoes and carrots in a large stockpot. Meanwhile, in another pot, boil cubed chicken for 8 minutes. Drain vegetables and chicken and set aside.

In a large skillet, sauté onion in butter until tender. Add flour, salt, thyme, and pepper, stirring until blended. Gradually stir in broth and milk. Bring to a boil; cook and stir for 2 minutes or until thickened. Add chicken, peas, corn, potatoes, and carrots. Remove from heat.

Crust Option 1
Line two 9-inch pie pans with bottom pastry; trim even with edge of pan. Fill pastry shells with chicken mixture. Roll out remaining pastry to fit top of pies. Cut slits or decorative cutouts in pastry. Place over filling; trim, seal, and style the edges. Bake one pot pie at 425°F for 35 to 40 minutes or until crust is lightly browned. Let stand for 15 minutes before cutting.

Crust Option 2
Mix together 2 cups biscuit/baking mix, 1¼ cups milk, 1 teaspoon garlic salt, and ½ teaspoon celery seed. (Mixture will be thin.) Spoon over top of chicken pot pie. Bake at 350°F for 30 to 35 minutes or until crust is golden brown. Cover and freeze remaining pot pie for up to 4 months.

To Serve
Cover edges of frozen pot pie with foil; place on a baking sheet. Bake at 425°F for 30 minutes. Reduce heat to 350°F and bake for 70 to 80 minutes longer, or until crust is golden brown.

Chicken Lime Taquitos

Yield: 36 taquitos

2 teaspoons salt
2 teaspoons chili powder
½ teaspoon garlic powder
¼ cup olive oil
¼ cup fresh lime juice
4 pounds boneless, skinless chicken
    breasts
1 teaspoon salt
2 teaspoons minced garlic
½ green pepper, sliced in long,
    thin strips
½ cup onion, sliced in long, thin
    strips
⅓ cup shredded cheddar cheese
2 tablespoons fresh lime juice
18 corn tortillas
3 cups canola or vegetable oil (for
    frying)
18 wooden toothpicks

In a large zip-top bag, mix together the first five ingredients. Add the chicken breasts and marinate for 2 hours in the refrigerator. (To use later, freeze the chicken breasts in the marinade.)

When you are ready to make the taquitos, defrost the chicken or take it out of the refrigerator. Drain off the liquid. Grill the chicken over medium-high heat until it is cooked through (about 6 minutes per side). Let the chicken cool slightly, then use your fingers to shred it into long, thin strips (about ⅛ inch by 3 inches).

Place cooked, shredded chicken in a bowl and sprinkle with ½ teaspoon salt and 2 teaspoons minced garlic. Mix well.

Add green pepper, onion, shredded cheese, and lime juice. Mix thoroughly.

To assemble, warm corn tortillas on a sprayed baking sheet in the oven at 350°F for 3 to 4 minutes until they are soft and pliable. Heat 3 cups oil in a skillet on high heat, then spoon ¼ cup chicken filling over each tortilla and roll tightly, securing with toothpick.

Deep-fry taquitos in oil at 350°F for 2 minutes or until golden brown and crispy. Drain well on a paper towel. When cool, place taquitos in a large zip-top bag in the freezer.

To Serve

Remove taquitos from freezer and place them on a foil-covered baking sheet. Bake taquitos in the oven at 425°F for 15 to 20 minutes or until warmed through and crisp. Serve with guacamole, sour cream, and/or salsa.

Chicken Enchiladas

Yield: two 9 x 13-inch pans (5 servings each)

3 cans (10¾ ounces each) cream of
   chicken soup
1 large container (24 ounces) sour
   cream
½ cup milk
1 can (14½ ounces) black beans
4 cups boneless, skinless chicken
   breast, cubed
1 cup fresh sliced mushrooms
1 small can (4 ounces) diced green
   chilies
1 cup chopped onions
2 teaspoons chili powder
1 teaspoon salt
1 teaspoon garlic powder
½ teaspoon pepper
20 flour tortillas
4 cups shredded cheddar cheese

In a medium bowl, combine the cream of chicken soup, sour cream, and milk, stirring until smooth. In a separate bowl, mix together the cubed chicken, black beans, mushrooms, chilies, onions, and seasonings. Fill 20 tortillas with the filling and place in two 9 x 13-inch foil pans, seam side down and tight together. Pour the sauce evenly over the enchiladas and top with cheese.

Pour ¼ cup water in the corners of each pan and cover pan with foil or layers of plastic wrap. Label "400°F, 1 hour" and freeze. If you want to serve one pan of enchiladas right away, bake it uncovered at 400°F for 30 minutes.

To Serve

Preheat oven to 400°F. Remove wrappings from frozen chicken enchiladas. Bake for 60 minutes or until chicken is cooked. Serve warm with chopped green lettuce, chips, and salsa.

Crunchy Chicken Tacos

Yield: 8 servings

3 eggs, lightly beaten
1½ cups seasoned breadcrumbs
¾ teaspoon salt
½ teaspoon pepper
12 chicken tenderloins

3 tablespoons canola oil
12 corn tortillas, toasted on a grill
1½ cups shredded cheddar cheese
toppings of choice (salsa, sour
    cream, guacamole, chopped
    tomatoes, black beans,
    shredded lettuce, fresh
    cilantro leaves)

Place beaten eggs in a shallow bowl. In another shallow bowl, combine breadcrumbs, salt, and pepper. Dip chicken tenderloins in eggs, then roll in breadcrumb mixture. In a large skillet over medium heat, cook chicken in oil for 4 to 5 minutes on each side or until juices run clear. Cool chicken and place on a lightly floured baking sheet in the freezer for one hour. When frozen, drop the battered chicken tenders into a large zip-top bag, label, and freeze. (Alternately, you can use store-bought pre-battered chicken tenders.)

To Serve
Place the frozen chicken tenders on a baking sheet and bake at 425°F for 18 to 20 minutes or until golden brown. Turn chicken pieces over halfway through the cooking process. Serve crunchy chicken pieces on toasted corn tortillas with cheese and toppings of choice.

Creamy Chicken Alfredo
Yield: 6 to 8 servings

2 packages Italian dressing mix*
1½ cups water
2 cans (10¾ ounces each) cream of
    chicken soup
2 packages (8 ounces each) cream cheese
2 to 3 tablespoons garlic powder
salt and pepper to taste
4 pounds boneless, skinless chicken
    breasts
1 package (12 ounces) penne pasta

Using a hand mixer, beat together the Italian dressing mix, water, cream of chicken soup, cream cheese, and garlic powder in a slow cooker.

Place the chicken in the slow cooker and cover it with sauce. Place lid on slow cooker and cook for 3 hours on LOW. Then whisk 1 cup of milk into the sauce to thin it. Place the cooked chicken breasts on a large cutting board and shred, using two forks. Stir the shredded chicken back into the sauce, then add salt and pepper to taste.

Meanwhile, cook pasta in boiling water until al dente (about 12 minutes). Rinse with cold water in a strainer. Freeze pasta on a floured baking sheet for 1 hour. Remove from freezer and place two cups of frozen pasta in each sandwich-size zip-top bag.

When the sauce is cool, place 2 cups in separate zip-top bags, then label bags and stack next to pasta bags in freezer.

To Serve

Defrost frozen sauce in microwave for 2 minutes on HIGH. Heat a skillet on medium-high heat. Remove plastic bags and drop one portion of frozen pasta and one portion of defrosted sauce into a skillet on the stovetop. Add 2 tablespoons water and cover with a lid. Cook for 10 to 15 minutes or until sauce is warm and creamy.

*If you don't have Italian dressing mix, make it from scratch using the recipe under "Emergency Substitutions."

Chicken Manicotti

Yield: three 8-inch square pans (4 servings each)

2 tablespoons garlic powder
1½ pounds boneless, skinless chicken breasts
2 boxes (8 ounces each) manicotti
4 to 5 cups bulk spaghetti sauce (see "Stock Your Freezer: Bulk Recipes")
1 pound Jimmy Dean Italian sausage, cooked and drained
4 cups (16 ounces) shredded mozzarella cheese
1 cup water, divided

Rub garlic powder over chicken; cut chicken into 1-inch strips. Stuff chicken into manicotti. Spread 1 cup spaghetti sauce in each of three greased 8-inch square foil pans.

Divide stuffed manicotti equally between three pans. Pour remaining spaghetti sauce over top. Be sure to cover all noodles or they will dry when cooked. Sprinkle with sausage and top with cheese.

Drizzle ⅓ cup water around the edge of each dish. Cover and bake one pan of manicotti at 375°F for 65 to 70 minutes or until chicken juices run clear and pasta is tender.

Cover, label "375°F, 70 minutes," and freeze remaining casseroles for up to 3 months.

To Serve

Thaw in refrigerator for 24 hours, then bake at 375°F for 65 to 70 minutes. To bake frozen, cover with foil and bake at 350°F for 2½ hours. Let sit for 15 minutes before serving.

Lime Herb Chicken

Yield: 8 servings

⅓ cup soy sauce
2 tablespoons lime zest
¼ cup fresh lime juice (you will need 3 or 4 limes)
1 tablespoon Worcestershire sauce
1 teaspoon ground mustard

2 tablespoons minced fresh oregano (or 2 teaspoons dried oregano)
3 garlic cloves, minced
1 teaspoon pepper
1 teaspoon paprika
6 boneless, skinless chicken breasts, cut into strips

In a large zip-top plastic bag, combine all ingredients. Seal and toss to coat, then label and freeze.

If serving right away, marinate chicken in refrigerator for at least 30 minutes. Place chicken on grill, or cook on a stovetop for 12 to 15 minutes (6 minutes each side) or until juices run clear.

To Serve

Defrost chicken in microwave. Place chicken on grill, or cook on a stovetop for 12 to 15 minutes (6 minutes each side) or until juices run clear. Marinade can be discarded or used as a sauce by bringing it to a boil on the stovetop and thickening it with 3 tablespoons cornstarch mixed into ½ cup cold water.

Helpful Hint

Preserve leftover lime peels in the freezer to use again. Just place them in a zip-top bag in the freezer. Lemon and orange peels freeze well too.

Chicken and Mushrooms with Saffron Rice

Yield: 8 to 10 servings

    2 pounds skinless, boneless chicken
        breasts
    3 tablespoons butter
    3 pounds fresh mushrooms (portobello or
        crimini), stemmed and sliced
    3 teaspoons chopped fresh rosemary
    3 teaspoons fresh minced or creamed garlic
    1½ cups low-sodium chicken stock
    1½ cups low-sodium beef stock
    1½ cups whipping cream
    pinch of saffron

Cut chicken into cubes, then boil it in a large pot of water for 10 minutes. Drain and set aside.

Melt butter in a skillet. Add mushrooms and rosemary. Do not stir. Let sit until mushrooms are tender and golden brown. Add garlic and sauté until you can smell it. Add stocks to the pan, bring to a boil, and reduce liquid by half.

Add whipping cream and reduce until thickened. Season to taste with fresh ground pepper and salt. Divide chicken into 4 to 5 large zip-top bags, then pour sauce over chicken pieces. Place each bag of chicken/sauce with a bag of frozen, cooked rice. Freeze up to 3 months.

To Serve
Defrost chicken/sauce in microwave and serve on a bed of hot rice.

For flavorful and colorful rice, rub a pinch of saffron in your hands to warm it, then sprinkle on rice. Cook rice on the stove in a covered saucepan. Do not remove or lift lid until rice is done, or the color will not be as bright.

Chicken Puffs

Yield: 8 to 10 servings

    2 packages refrigerator crescent rolls
    2 cups crushed buttery crackers
        (I use Ritz)
    2½ cups cubed cooked chicken
    ¼ cup diced onion
    ½ cup chopped celery
    4 ounces (½ package) cream cheese
    ½ cup sour cream

dash garlic powder

dash salt and pepper

Press together 2 crescent-roll triangles to form a square. Repeat with remaining dough. Place crushed crackers in a shallow dish. Stir together remaining ingredients in a large bowl and scoop by heaping teaspoonfuls onto dough squares.

Fold and pinch edges together. Roll each chicken puff in the cracker crumbs. Place puffs on a greased cookie sheet and put cookie sheet in freezer for 1 hour. Then place chicken puffs in a zip-top freezer bag and freeze.

To Serve
Place frozen chicken puffs on a greased cookie sheet and bake at 350°F for 20 to 30 minutes or until golden brown.

Chicken Cordon Bleu
Yield: 8 Servings

1 bottle (12 ounces) Lawry's 30-
    minute marinade (herb and garlic) or a
    homemade marinade (see
    "Emergency Substitutions")
8 boneless, skinless chicken breasts
8 slices Swiss or pepper Jack cheese

8 slices ham, cut in half

¼ cup (½ stick) butter, melted

2 cups Italian breadcrumbs

Trim the fat off the chicken breasts. Butterfly each chicken breast (slice it so it opens up into 2 large, flat pieces). Each breast will make 2 chicken cordon bleu portions, which equals 1 serving.

Divide chicken breasts in 2 large zip-top bags and pour in marinade. Marinate for at least 15 minutes; for best results, marinate overnight.

After marinating, leave chicken in the bags while you use a meat mallet or heavy pan to pound and flatten the chicken until it is ¼ inch thick.

Lay out 2 shallow dishes, 8 toothpicks, a cookie sheet, and a paper towel. Melt butter in one shallow dish; pour breadcrumbs in the other. Place paper towel on cookie sheet.

Remove chicken from bags, then lay it out on the plastic wrap. Place ½ slice of cheese and ½ slice of ham on each chicken breast.

Roll chicken up like a burrito while tucking the meat and cheese in the middle. Secure with a toothpick. Don't worry about tucking in the sides; the cheese will ooze out and get crispy in the pan. Dip in butter, then roll in breadcrumbs. Place on a paper towel and place in the freezer for 1 hour.

Place frozen uncooked chicken in a large zip-top bag, label "Chicken Cordon Bleu, 325°F, 35 minutes," and freeze.

To Serve

Place frozen chicken cordon bleu on a foil-covered cookie sheet in the oven at 325°F for 35 minutes. Cut into one piece of chicken to see if it is cooked all the way through. Once chicken is done, remove it from the oven and set it on a plate with a piece of foil (in tent shape) over the top so juices will flow back into all areas of the meat. Serve chicken warm with vegetables and breadsticks.

Hawaiian Haystacks

Yield: 16 servings

4 cans (10¾ ounces each) cream of chicken soup

4 cups boneless, skinless chicken, cubed and cooked
2 soup cans (10¾ ounces each) water or broth
2 bay leaves
8 cups cooked long-grain rice
topping choices (pineapple tidbits, chopped green onions, green peppers, celery, cooked chicken [cut into bite size pieces], cooked rice, sliced water chestnuts, grated cheddar cheese, fried chow mein noodles, toasted almonds [slivered], diced or sliced tomatoes, shredded coconut)

To make the gravy, combine the soup and water or broth in a medium saucepan. Stir to blend. Add cubed chicken and bay leaves. Simmer for 10 to 15 minutes or until heated through. Place gravy in zip-top bags, label, and freeze.

To Serve

Warm the chicken gravy and rice in the microwave. Chop all the toppings and set them in individual bowls. To serve, layer on plates by stacking first the rice, then the chow mein noodles, then the toppings, and then the chicken gravy.

Hawaiian Teriyaki Chicken

Yield: 6 to 8 servings

2 cups soy sauce
2 cups water
2 cups brown sugar, firmly packed
2 cups sugar
1 teaspoon sesame oil
1 tablespoon minced ginger
1 green onion, chopped
3 garlic cloves, minced
3 pounds chicken tenders or breasts,
　　sliced into 1-inch strips

Place all ingredients except chicken into 2 large zip-top bags. Stir to create marinade. Squeeze all the air out of the bags. Label and freeze. (Marinate the meat for at least 15 minutes in the fridge, or up to 3 months in the freezer.)

To Serve

Defrost frozen meat in the microwave and then cook in a hot skillet for 5 minutes on each side. Serve with rice. To turn marinade into a sauce, bring it to a boil on the stove and add 3 tablespoons cornstarch mixed with ½ cup cold water. (Mix the cornstarch with water before pouring it into the sauce or it will be lumpy.) Stir until sauce thickens, and then pour on rice.

Another option is to place all ingredients in a slow cooker and cook on LOW for 3 hours. Serve with rice and freeze leftovers.

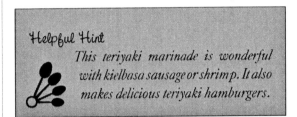

Helpful Hint
This teriyaki marinade is wonderful with kielbasa sausage or shrimp. It also makes delicious teriyaki hamburgers.

Orange Chicken

Yield: 8 servings

This dish tastes similar to the orange chicken at a popular Chinese fast-food restaurant chain. There is a quick way to make it, or a from-scratch method that takes a little more time.

Quick Method

3 pounds pre-battered chicken tenders
3 cups frozen cooked rice

Orange Sauce

    3 tablespoons soy sauce

    ⅓ cup water

    ⅔ cup sugar

    ⅔ cup white vinegar

    3 tablespoons cornstarch mixed
        into ½ cup cold water (mix
        together before pouring into
        sauce mixture)

    1 tablespoon orange zest (grate the
        peel, avoiding the white part)

Bake battered chicken at 425°F for 18 minutes. Heat frozen cooked rice in the microwave for 4 to 5 minutes on HIGH.

In a small saucepan, combine ingredients for orange sauce and cook over medium heat until thickened. Pour over chicken and garnish with orange zest. Serve immediately with rice.

Battered Chicken from Scratch

Always marinate meat before cooking it. Salt and pepper will dry meat out but a marinade tenderizes and adds flavor. You can marinate as little as 15 minutes before use.

    2 pounds boneless, skinless chicken

Marinade:

    2 tablespoons soy sauce

    2 tablespoons rice vinegar or apple
        cider vinegar

    2 teaspoons sesame oil

    2 teaspoons cornstarch

Batter:

    ⅔ cup all-purpose flour

    ⅔ cup cornstarch

    2 egg whites, lightly beaten

    2 tablespoons canola or vegetable oil

    ⅔ cup warm water, as needed

Cut chicken into 2-inch cubes, then marinate for at least 15 minutes. Heat 3 cups vegetable oil on high heat in a skillet or deep-fat fryer (lighter-colored oils can be used for cooking at high temperature).

In a large bowl, combine flour and cornstarch. Then stir in egg whites and oil. Add as much of the warm water as needed to form a thick batter.

Stir chicken pieces in batter until they are completely covered on all sides. (If using previously frozen chicken, pat dry before placing in batter.)

Drop each piece of battered chicken into the oil *one at a time* so they don't stick together. Only place about 10 pieces at a time in the hot oil. Fry chicken pieces for 4 to 5 minutes, until they are a light golden brown and float to the top. Set on a paper towel to drain off excess oil.

Freeze fried chicken pieces on a lightly floured baking sheet for 1 hour. Take out of the freezer and drop all fried chicken pieces in a large zip-top bag. Freeze for up to 6 months.

Sweet and Sour Sauce

Yield: 2 cups (6 servings)

¼ cup sugar
2 tablespoons ketchup
2 tablespoons soy sauce
¼ teaspoon salt
½ cup water or reserved pineapple juice
¼ cup white vinegar
2 tablespoons cornstarch dissolved in ½ cup water
1 carrot, thinly sliced lengthwise

½ green pepper, chopped
½ cup pineapple tidbits

To Serve

Mix together the first 6 ingredients. Bring to a boil in a small saucepan over medium heat. Add carrots, pepper, and pineapple. Bring to a boil again and pour in cornstarch mixture. Stir until thickened. Pour sauce over baked battered chicken and serve hot.

Sweet and Savory Chicken Wings

Yield: 8 servings

24 whole chicken wings (about 5 pounds)
1½ cups barbecue sauce
1½ cups honey
1½ cups soy sauce

Cut chicken wings into three sections. Remove and discard the wing-tip section.

Divide barbecue sauce, honey, and soy sauce into two large zip-top bags. Place half of the wings in each bag, then close bag tightly and make sure wings are covered with marinade. Label each bag and freeze.

To Serve

Remove chicken wings from the freezer and defrost in the microwave for 2 minutes. Do not drain the liquid. Preheat oven to 350°F and place chicken wings and liquid in a greased 9 x 13-inch baking dish. Bake, uncovered, at 350°F for 50 to 60 minutes or until chicken juices run clear. Serve with carrots, celery, and blue cheese dressing or over rice.

Spicy Hot Wings

Yield: 8 servings

    3 pounds chicken wing
        drumettes
    ½ cup (1 stick) butter
    ½ cup ground fresh chili
        paste or hot pepper sauce
    3 teaspoons dried rosemary, crushed
    2 teaspoons dried thyme
    ½ teaspoon paprika
    ½ teaspoon salt
    ½ teaspoon garlic powder

In a large, resealable plastic bag, melt the butter and then add the hot pepper sauce and seasonings. Add wings; toss to evenly coat. Label and freeze chicken drumettes for up to 3 months.

To Serve

Defrost the chicken in the microwave, drain off any excess water, and transfer to a foil-lined 9 x 13-inch baking dish. Bake, uncovered, at 425°F for 30 minutes or until chicken juices run clear. Serve wings hot with celery sticks and blue cheese dressing on the side.

Barbecue Ranch Chicken Salad

Yield: 10 servings

    1 pound boneless, skinless
        chicken breasts, cut into
        ⅓-inch strips
    1 teaspoon chili powder
    1 tablespoon vegetable oil
    1 can (14½ ounces) black
        beans, drained
    1 can (14½ ounces) corn,
        drained

¼ cup diced red onion

1 medium tomato, diced

1 small cucumber, seeded and
finely diced

⅓ cup ranch salad dressing

¼ cup salsa

¼ cup barbecue sauce

1 cup (4 ounces) shredded cheddar
cheese

1 package (16 ounces) ready-to-
serve green salad

1 bag tortilla chips

Sprinkle chicken strips with chili powder. In a skillet, cook chicken in oil for 6 minutes or until juices run clear. Use a fork to shred the cooked chicken on a cutting board.

In a large bowl, mix together corn, black beans, tomato, cucumber, and diced red onion. Add shredded chicken, then place in zip-top bags, label, and freeze.

To Serve

Warm the chicken mixture in microwave and drain off any extra liquid. Mix in ranch dressing and barbecue sauce and then add the shredded cheese. Stir to coat. Add this mixture to the ready-to-serve green salad and stir. Top this salad with more shredded cheese and serve with tortilla chips.

White Chicken Chili

Yield: 6 servings

1 medium onion, chopped

2 garlic cloves, minced

1 pinch red chili pepper flakes

1 tablespoon vegetable oil

4 cups chicken broth

2 cans (14½ ounces each) great northern
beans, rinsed and drained

2 tablespoons minced fresh parsley

1 tablespoon lime juice

1 to 1¼ teaspoons ground cumin

1 tablespoon soy sauce

2 tablespoons cornstarch

¼ cup cold water

2 pounds cubed cooked chicken (see
"Stock Your Freezer: Bulk Recipes")

toppings (see "To Serve")

In a large saucepan, cook the onion, red pepper flakes, and garlic in oil until tender.

Stir in the broth, beans, parsley, lime juice, soy sauce, and cumin; bring to a boil. Reduce heat; cover and simmer for 10 minutes, stirring occasionally.

Combine cornstarch and water and stir until smooth; stir into chili. Add chicken. Bring to a boil; cook and stir for 2 minutes or until thickened.

Divide and freeze in small zip-top bags for 3 to 6 months.

To Serve

Defrost in microwave until warm. Serve on rice or chips topped with shredded cheese, diced tomatoes, and sour cream.

Parmesan-Crusted Chicken and Broccoli

Yield: two 9 x 13-inch pans (6 to 8 servings each)

2 pounds chopped cooked chicken (see "Stock Your Freezer: Bulk Recipes")

2 pounds broccoli
5 cup cooked rice (see "Stock Your Freezer: Bulk Recipes")

Sauce

4 cans (10¾ ounces each) cream of chicken soup
2 cups (16 ounces) sour cream
½ cup milk
1 teaspoon onion powder (or ½ medium onion, diced)

Topping (Per Pan)

2 packages crushed buttery crackers, such as Ritz brand
4 tablespoons (½ stick) butter
4 teaspoons garlic salt
4 teaspoons dried parsley
¾ cup grated Parmesan cheese

Steam broccoli in microwave for 6 minutes. Cube chicken and cook for 6 minutes in microwave on HIGH. In a medium bowl, blend the sauce ingredients. Spread cooked rice in each 9 x 13-inch pan. Divide half the sauce between the two pans and pour over the rice. Top the sauce with broccoli, then chicken, and then the remaining sauce.

Mix topping in a zip-top plastic bag and sprinkle on top of both casseroles. Wrap casseroles in plastic wrap, label "350°F, 30 minutes, or 1 hour frozen," and freeze.

To Serve

If casserole is frozen, remove plastic wrap and bake at 350°F for 1 hour. Or defrost casserole for 24 hours in refrigerator and then bake at 350°F for 40 minutes or until warmed all the way through.

Creamy Chicken and Rice Bake

Yield: two 9 x 13-inch pans (8 servings each)

    8 boneless, skinless chicken breasts
    6 cups cooked rice
    2 boxes (6 ounces each) stuffing mix
    2 cans (10¾ ounces each) cream of
        chicken soup
    2 cups sour cream
    2 cups milk

Press 4 cups of cooked rice into the bottom of each pan. Slice the chicken breasts into 1-inch by 3-inch slices and place on top of the rice. In a large bowl, mix together the cream of chicken soup, sour cream, and milk. Pour over chicken and rice, then top with stuffing mix. Bake 1 pan at 350°F for 1 hour and wrap the other in plastic wrap. Label "350°F, 1 hour frozen."

To Serve

Preheat oven to 350°F. Bake frozen chicken and rice for 1 hour or until chicken is cooked and sauce is warm. Serve warm with rolls and a vegetable.

Garlic Lemon Chicken

Yield: 8 servings

    4 cups lemon juice
    4 cups water
    15 garlic cloves, crushed
    1 cup dijon or yellow mustard
    3 tablespoons lemon pepper (or salt and
        pepper to taste)
    16 chicken thighs

In a food processor, combine the lemon juice, water, garlic, and mustard. Divide into two large zip-top bags and add the chicken. Freeze the chicken in the marinade at least overnight.

To Serve

Defrost the chicken thighs in the microwave or let sit in refrigerator overnight. Heat grill to medium-high and grill the chicken until it is cooked through (about 6 minutes per side). Serve with sweet black beans and rice.

Roasted Chicken

Yield: 8 cups shredded chicken

  3 tablespoons fresh rosemary, finely
    chopped
  2 tablespoons fresh sage leaves, finely
    chopped
  4 garlic cloves, chopped
  1 tablespoon salt
  5 tablespoons olive oil
  1 large whole chicken (4 to 5 pounds)
  1 small bottle (12 ounces) white wine
  2 cups baby carrots
  10 fingerling potatoes
  1 onion, sliced
  3 bay leaves
  1 bundle of thyme (10 sprigs tied
    together with string)

In a small bowl, combine rosemary, sage, garlic, red pepper flakes, and olive oil. Take this mixture and slide it under the skin of the chicken. Move your fingertips carefully along the underside of the skin to detach it from the meat, being careful not to tear the skin. Once the herbs are under the skin, drizzle the bird with olive oil, sprinkle it with salt, and massage the bird so all the skin is oiled and salted. Tie the bird's legs together with string so it will keep its shape. Preheat oven to 450°F.

Pour white wine into a 2-inch-deep baking pan, then add the carrots, potatoes, and onion slices. Tuck in 3 bay leaves plus the bundle of thyme. Place the bird on top of the veggies, feet facing down.

Bake the chicken for 15 minutes, then lower the oven temperature to 375°F. Cook the bird for another 45 minutes, turning it every 15 minutes to brown the skin on all sides.

Use a thermometer to check the temperature of the chicken between the thigh and the breast. When the temperature reaches 160 to 170°F, the meat is done. If it is not quite there, cook for an additional 10 minutes. After removing the chicken from the oven, let it rest for 10 minutes. Then carve the meat, shred it, and place it in zip-top freezer bags, about 2 cups of chicken in each. Label and freeze.

Savory Thanksgiving Turkey

Defrost time: 24 hours
Marinate time: 24 hours
Yield: 10 servings

> 1 six- to seven-pound frozen
>   turkey
> 3 quarts (12 cups) water
> 2 cups salt
> 1½ cups brown sugar, firmly
>   packed
> 2 tablespoons dried rosemary
> 2 tablespoons dried thyme
> 1 oven bag

Defrost turkey in refrigerator for 24 hours. In a large stockpot, combine all ingredients except for the turkey and oven bag. Bring to a boil on the stove.

Remove boiling water from the stove and cool. Place defrosted turkey in the stockpot and let it marinate for 24 hours in refrigerator.

After the turkey marinates, take out the innards (neck and plastic sack containing liver and giblets) and rinse the turkey with water.

Cover turkey with melted butter and sprinkle with rosemary and thyme. Lightly dust the inside of an oven bag with flour, then place turkey inside.

Cook turkey at 350°F for 2½ hours, or according to directions on oven bag.

To carve the turkey, cut off wings and drumsticks, then slice turkey into ¾-inch-thick pieces. Cube leftover turkey and freeze for turkey meals. (See Index.)

Turkey and Stuffing Bake

Yield: three 9 x 13-inch pans (8 to 10 servings each)

> 3 packages (6 ounces each) stuffing mix
> 10 to 11 cups cubed cooked turkey (or
>   chicken)
> 2 cups (8 ounces) shredded cheddar cheese
> 2 cans (10¾ ounces) cream of celery soup
> 2 cans (10¾ ounces) cream of chicken
>   soup

1 can (10¾ ounces) cream of
mushroom soup
1 can (12 ounces) evaporated milk
1½ cups (6 ounces) shredded Swiss
cheese
salt and pepper to taste

Prepare stuffing mix according to package directions. Add turkey and cheddar cheese. Combine the soups and milk in a separate bowl.

Pour 1 cup soup mixture into each of three greased 9 x 13-inch foil baking dishes. Top with turkey mixture and remaining soup mixture. Sprinkle with Swiss cheese. Cover and freeze 2 casseroles for up to 3 months.

Cover and bake the remaining casserole at 350°F for 30 to 35 minutes or until bubbly. Let stand for 5 to 10 minutes before serving.

To Serve
Bake, frozen and uncovered, at 350°F for 90 minutes or until bubbly. Or defrost overnight in the fridge and bake at 350°F for 35 to 40 minutes. Let stand for 5 to 10 minutes before serving.

Cheesy Turkey Bake
Yield: two 9-inch square pans (4 to 6 servings each)
2 cups chicken stock or broth
2 cups water
4 teaspoons dried minced onion
2 cups uncooked rice
2 cups frozen peas, thawed
4 cups cubed cooked turkey
2 cans (10¾ ounces each) cheddar cheese
soup
2 cups milk
1 teaspoons salt
2 cups finely crushed butter-flavored
crackers (about 60)
5 tablespoons (about ⅔ stick butter),
melted

In a large saucepan, bring the stock, water, and minced onion to a boil. Reduce heat. Add rice; cover and simmer for 15 minutes. Remove from heat; fluff with a fork. Divide rice between two greased 9-inch square baking pans. Sprinkle each with peas and turkey.

In a bowl, combine soup, milk, and salt, stirring until smooth; pour over turkey. Toss cracker crumbs and butter; sprinkle over top. Cover and freeze 1 casserole for up to 3 months. Bake remaining casserole, uncovered, at 350°F for 35 minutes or until golden brown.

To Serve

Thaw in refrigerator for 24 hours. Bake, uncovered, at 350°F for 65 minutes or until heated through. Or bake frozen for 2 hours.

Beef

Beef and Broccoli Stir-fry

Yield: 8 servings

> 2 to 3 pounds frozen sirloin strips (see
> "Stock Your Freezer: Bulk Recipes")
> 2 to 3 pounds frozen broccoli

Sauce
> 4 tablespoons soy sauce
> 4 teaspoons balsamic vinegar
> 4 teaspoons brown sugar
> 4 garlic cloves, minced

Microwave frozen sirloin strips in a microwave-safe bowl for 3 to 4 minutes on HIGH until defrosted. Pat dry with a paper towel.

Heat 1 tablespoon canola or vegetable oil in a large skillet and pan-fry beef strips for 3 to 4 minutes. Remove beef from skillet and set aside. Cover with an aluminum-foil tent to allow juices to flow back into meat.

Heat 1 tablespoon oil on medium-high heat. Add broccoli and 1 tablespoon water. Cover and let cook until steamed (about 5 minutes). Add cooked sirloin and stir in sauce.

To Serve

Remove beef, broccoli, and sauce mixture from heat. Serve over hot rice.

Ginger Sirloin Strips

Yield: 8 servings

> 2 pounds frozen sirloin strips (see
> "Stock Your Freezer:
> Bulk Recipes")
> 2 cans (14 ounces each) pineapple tidbits
> (drained, reserve juice)
> 2 cans (11 ounces each) mandarin
> oranges (drained, reserve juice)
> 4 tablespoons cornstarch
> 3 tablespoons minced ginger
> 2 cups thinly sliced green onions
> hot cooked rice

Defrost beef strips in microwave for 3 to 4 minutes on HIGH in a microwave-safe dish.

In a large skillet, stir-fry beef and ginger in 1 tablespoon canola oil until meat is no longer pink. Add onions and pineapple. Stir cornstarch into saved juice and add to skillet. Cook and stir until slightly thickened. Gently stir in oranges. Serve with rice.

To add more color to the dish, add a can of whole cranberries along with the pineapple.

Lasagna Roll-Ups

Yield: two 9 x 13-inch foil pans (8 servings each)

    1 box (16 ounces) lasagna noodles, cooked
    1 large container (24 ounces) cottage
        cheese
    2 teaspoons minced fresh chives
    2 teaspoons dried oregano
    2 teaspoons dried basil
    1 package (3.5 ounces or about
        48 slices) pepperoni
    16 slices Swiss cheese, cut into thirds
    3 cans (26 ounces each) meatless
        spaghetti sauce
    1 cup shredded Parmesan cheese

Boil lasagna noodles according to package directions; drain. Combine cottage cheese, chives, oregano, and basil.

Lay noodles out flat on a cutting board or baking sheet. Spread ¼ cup cottage cheese mixture on each noodle within ½ inch of edges. Top with 2 to 3 slices of pepperoni and 2 slices of pre-cut Swiss cheese; carefully roll up.

Place seam side down in two large greased 9 x 13-inch foil baking dishes; top with spaghetti sauce. Cover pans in foil, wrap in a few layers of plastic wrap, label, and freeze.

To Serve

Bake frozen lasagna roll-ups, covered, at 350°F for 60 minutes or until sauce is bubbly. Uncover and bake for 5 more minutes. Sprinkle with Parmesan cheese. Bake until cheese is melted. Let stand for 5 minutes before serving.

Lasagna

Yield: two 9 x 13-inch pans (8 servings each)

- 1 box (16 ounces) regular lasagna
  noodles (do not precook)
- 4 cups grated mozzarella cheese
- 1 container (24 ounces) cottage or
  ricotta cheese
- 1 package (8 ounces) cream cheese
- ½ cup Parmesan cheese
- 10 cups bulk spaghetti sauce (see
  "Stock Your Freezer: Bulk
  Recipes")

In 2 greased 9 x 13-inch aluminum pans, layer ingredients in the following order:

- 3 noodles
- cottage or ricotta cheese
- mozzarella cheese
- nickel-sized bits of cream cheese,
  distributed evenly over sauce

Repeat layers. Do not overfill or sauce will spill over in oven while baking.

Wrap pans with foil, label "350°F, 45 minutes, or if frozen, 350°F, 2 hours," and freeze.

To Serve

Bake frozen at 350°F for 2 hours, or thaw overnight in refrigerator and bake at 350°F for 45 minutes. Remove cover for final 10 minutes. Let stand 10 minutes before serving so that excess water can soak back into the noodles.

Cheesy Ravioli

Yield: three 9 x 13-inch pans (8 servings each)

- 3 bags (13 ounces each) frozen cheese
  ravioli
- 10 cups bulk spaghetti sauce (see
  "Stock Your Freezer: Bulk
  Recipes")
- 3 cups mozzarella cheese

Make bulk spaghetti sauce and freeze in 3 separate doubled freezer bags. Freeze sauce flat and place a frozen cheese ravioli bag next to it.

To Serve

Defrost 4 to 5 cups of bulk spaghetti sauce. Sauce must be completely defrosted to cook correctly.

Boil frozen ravioli for 5 minutes. Pour ½ cup sauce on bottom of a 9 x 13-inch foil pan. Drain ravioli, then place in pan. Completely cover ravioli with remaining sauce and sprinkle mozzarella cheese on top.

Cover top of the pan with foil; bake at 350°F for 30 minutes. Uncover and cook 10 more minutes. Let stand 10 minutes before serving.

Beef Fajitas
Yield: 8 servings

    1 green pepper, cut into ¼-inch strips
    1 red pepper, cut into ¼-inch strips
    1 yellow pepper, cut into ¼-inch strips
    1 medium onion, thinly sliced
    2 pounds sirloin strips (see "Stock
        Your Freezer: Bulk Recipes")
    ¾ cup water
    fajita- or soft taco-size flour tortillas
    ½ cup A-1 Steak Sauce
    2 tablespoons red wine vinegar
    1 tablespoon lime juice
    1 teaspoon ground cumin
    1 teaspoon chili powder
    1 teaspoon salt
    1 teaspoon garlic powder

    ½ teaspoon pepper
    ½ teaspoon cayenne pepper
    toppings (salsa, shredded cheese, sour
        cream, and cilantro)

In the microwave, defrost sirloin strips just until they break apart. Place strips in slow cooker. Add sliced onion and peppers.

Combine water, vinegar, lime juice, and seasonings. Pour over meat in slow cooker. Cover and cook on LOW for 8 to 9 hours or until tender. Freeze in quart-size zip-top freezer bags.

To Serve
Reheat fajita mixture in microwave. Place meat mixture down the center of each tortilla. Top each with salsa, shredded cheese, sour cream, and cilantro; roll up.

Chimichangas
Yield: 6 servings

    2 pounds taco meat, defrosted (see "Stock
        Your Freezer: Bulk Recipes")
    1 pound bulk refried beans, defrosted
    2 cups cheese
    12 flour tortillas

Optional Toppings
  1 cup salsa
  2 cups chopped lettuce
  1 avocado, sliced
  6 olives (for garnish)
  1 cup sour cream

Defrost taco meat and refried beans in the microwave until warm. (Another great filler for chimichangas is chili verde.) Place desired amount of meat and beans in each flour tortilla, then sprinkle with cheese. Tuck sides of tortilla in first, then roll up and seal the seam with a toothpick.

Heat 1 cup canola or vegetable oil in a hot skillet on medium-high heat. When oil is hot, place 4 or 5 chimichangas in hot oil, seam side down. Turn chimichangas when golden brown on bottom. Brown the other side and then place on a paper towel.

To Serve
Pull out toothpicks and place chimichangas on a bed of lettuce and other toppings. Serve warm. Freeze leftover chimichangas. Bake frozen at 425°F for 11 to 15 minutes, or until golden brown and heated through.

Sweet Sloppy Joe Mix
Yield: 10 servings

  2 pounds lean ground beef
  ½ cup chopped onion
  ½ cup chopped green bell pepper
  2 teaspoons prepared yellow mustard
  1½ cups ketchup
  1 tablespoon brown sugar
  1 teaspoon garlic powder
  salt and pepper to taste

In a medium skillet over medium heat, brown the ground beef with the onion and green pepper; drain liquid.

Stir in the garlic powder, mustard, ketchup, and brown sugar; mix thoroughly. Reduce heat and simmer for 30 minutes.

Season with salt and pepper. Serve right away on hamburger buns or freeze in sandwich-size zip top bags.

To Serve

Defrost sloppy joe mixture in the microwave or on the stove over medium heat. Serve on hamburger buns with carrot sticks and chips.

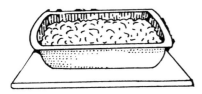

Chili and Cornbread Bake

Yield: two 9 x 13-inch pans (8 servings each)

2 pounds ground beef
2 large onions, chopped
2 cans (14½ ounces each) black
    beans, drained
4 cups frozen corn (or one 15-ounce can)
2 cans (15 ounces each) tomato sauce
2 cans (14½ ounces each) diced
    tomatoes, undrained
½ cup bacon, chopped (optional; see
    "Stock Your Freezer: Bulk Recipes")
4 teaspoons chili powder
2 teaspoons salt
4 teaspoons ground cumin
1 teaspoon sugar
1 teaspoon garlic powder

Cornbread Topping
    1 cup all-purpose flour
    1 cup cornmeal
    2 teaspoons baking powder
    ⅛ teaspoon salt
    1 egg
    ½ cup milk
    ½ cup sour cream
    ⅓ cup frozen corn

In a large pot over medium heat, combine all chili ingredients. Bring to a boil, then reduce heat and cover. Simmer for 10 minutes.

In a medium bowl, combine all the ingredients for the cornbread topping except corn. Beat until smooth, stir in corn, and mix until just moistened.

Pour chili into 2 ungreased 9 x 13-inch baking dishes. Drop cornbread by heaping teaspoonfuls onto chili.

Bake 1 pan at 400°F for 17 minutes or until bread is lightly browned. Wrap the other pan in plastic wrap and label "400°F, 30 minutes," then freeze.

To Serve

Take frozen chili and cornbread out of the freezer and remove plastic wrap. Bake frozen at 400°F for 30 minutes.

Chili 'n' Tots

Yield: two 8-inch square casseroles (6 servings each)

- 1 pound ground beef (see "Stock Your Freezer: Bulk Recipes")
- 2 cans (15 ounces each) chili
- 1 can (8 ounces) tomato sauce
- 1 can (2¼ ounces) sliced ripe olives, drained
- 2 cups (8 ounces) shredded cheddar cheese
- 1 package (32 ounces) Tater Tots brand frozen potato nuggets

Defrost precooked ground beef in microwave. Stir in chili, tomato sauce, and olives. Transfer to two greased 8-inch square foil pans. Sprinkle with cheese; top with tots.

Cover and freeze one casserole for up to 3 months. Cover and bake remaining casserole at 350°F for 35 to 40 minutes or until heated through.

To Serve

Remove from freezer, cover, and bake at 350°F for 1½ hours or until heated through.

My Favorite Meatballs

Yield: 20 meatballs

- 1 large onion, finely diced
- 1 cup seasoned breadcrumbs
- ½ cup water
- 2 garlic cloves, minced
- 1½ pounds lean ground beef
- 2 tablespoons parsley flakes
- 1 cup grated Parmigian-Reggiano cheese
- 2 large eggs
- 2 teaspoons salt

Preheat oven to 350°F. In a hot skillet, sauté diced onions with olive oil until translucent (about 5 minutes). Add garlic and sauté another 2 minutes. Remove from heat and cool.

In a large bowl, mix together meat, eggs, cheese, parsley, and breadcrumbs. Add onions and season with salt. Use your hands to thoroughly mix. Add water. (The mixture should be quite wet.) Sprinkle on more salt, then shape into golf ball-size portions.

Place meatballs in a hot skillet and brown all sides. Place browned meatballs on a cookie sheet and bake for about 15 minutes. Cool and use some right away and freeze the rest on a cookie sheet for 1 hour. Then place frozen meatballs in a zip-top bag, label, and freeze.

To Serve
Warm meatballs in microwave and serve with spaghetti sauce, or as an appetizer with barbecue sauce.

Sirloin Tips with Mushroom Gravy

Yield: 12 servings

1 package fresh mushrooms, sliced (or two 8-ounce cans sliced mushrooms)
2 tablespoons (¼ stick) butter
3-pound sirloin tip roast, trimmed, cut into ½-inch cubes
1 packet onion soup mix (see "Emergency Substitutions" to make soup mix from scratch)
1 can (10¾ ounces) cream of chicken soup
1 can (15 ounces) low-sodium beef broth (or 1½ cups water with 2 beef bouillon cubes)

Sauté fresh mushrooms in a skillet with 2 tablespoons hot butter (do not stir; just let mushrooms sit for about 10 minutes, then flip and brown the other side).

Place cubed beef in slow cooker (use slow-cooker liner for easy cleanup). Stir in remaining ingredients. Cover and cook on LOW for 6 hours. Serve over cooked rice, pasta, or mashed potatoes.

Cool remaining beef and gravy. Place in zip-top bags, label "Sirloin Tips and Gravy," and freeze.

To Serve
Defrost sirloin tips and gravy in a microwave-safe bowl on HIGH until warm. Serve over previously frozen mashed potatoes (see "Stock Your Freezer: Bulk Recipes"), or with vegetable of choice.

Pork

Pot Stickers

Yield: 10 to 12 appetizer-size servings

2 packages round wonton wrappers
(2-inch circles)
2 cups thinly sliced Napa or bok
choy cabbage (diced sweet
potato works as well)
1½ pounds uncooked ground
pork sausage
4 teaspoons minced fresh or
bottled ginger
1 green onion, finely chopped
2 teaspoons soy sauce

Dice cabbage into very small pieces. Discard the rest of the cabbage or use in a soup.

In a large bowl, combine all ingredients except wonton wrappers, mixing well with hands.

Lightly flour 2 cookie sheets. Put some water in a small bowl to dip your fingers in. Wet one side of a wonton wrapper and spoon 2 teaspoons filling on the center of the wrapper. Fold in half like a taco and pinch edges closed. If the edges don't seal, wet them with your fingers and pinch edges until they seal. Continue filling wonton wrappers until sausage mixture is gone.

Place pot stickers on a lightly floured cookie sheet and freeze for 1 to 2 hours. Then put frozen pot stickers into a large zip-top freezer bag. Pull out pot stickers as needed.

To Serve*

Heat 2 tablespoons canola oil in a nonstick skillet, then place frozen wontons in the skillet on high heat. Add 3 tablespoons water and cover with lid to steam the pot stickers. Cook until liquid is gone, about 7 or 8 minutes.

When pot stickers turn brown and crispy on one side, flip them over and cook the other side until it is brown and crispy. If you flip them too early, they will stick to the pan. Serve pot stickers hot with dipping sauce.

*A more healthy way to cook pot stickers is to drop them into a pot of boiling water. When they float to the top, they are done. Serve hot with dipping sauce.

Dipping Sauce for Pot Stickers

Yield: 1½ cups (6 servings)

6 tablespoons soy sauce
6 tablespoons water
6 tablespoons balsamic vinegar
2 tablespoons brown sugar
6 garlic cloves, minced

Combine ingredients and divide sauce into six small bowls—one for each person to dip pot stickers in. For a spicy sauce, add 1 teaspoon hot sauce or chili pepper flakes.

Glazed Polish Dogs

Yield: 6 to 8 servings

8 frozen Polish dogs
½ cup brown sugar
½ cup (1 stick) butter

In a saucepan, melt the butter. Then stir in the brown sugar and bring to a boil.

Defrost Polish dogs, slice in half lengthwise, and place in the sauce. Turn down the heat and simmer the Polish dogs for 20 minutes.

Take Polish dogs out of glaze and grill or broil just until lightly browned.

Barbecued Pulled-Pork Sandwiches

Yield: 8 to 10 servings

3-pound pork roast
5 to 6 whole cloves
1 tablespoon dried rosemary (optional)
1 medium onion, chopped (optional)
2 cups water
1 bottle (28 ounces) barbecue sauce
    (I use Sweet Baby Ray's)
salt and pepper to taste

Trim the fat off the pork roast. Place first 5 ingredients in the slow cooker. (Be sure to use a slow-cooker liner for easier cleanup.) Cook on LOW for 8 to 12 hours or overnight.

Drain liquid, remove cloves, and shred pork with 2 forks. Be sure to remove any fat chunks. Stir in barbecue sauce, then add salt and pepper to taste.

After meat cools, place it in sandwich-size zip-top freezer bags. I like to put my shredded pork next to my frozen garlic mashed potatoes (see "Stock Your Freezer: Bulk Recipes") so they are easy to grab for a meal.

To Serve

Defrost in microwave. Serve shredded pork on toasted dinner rolls or toasted, buttered bread.

Cheesy Ham Bake

Yield: two 9 x 13-inch pans (8 servings each)

    1 package (13 to 16 ounces) rotini,
        or any other small, sturdy pasta
    2 cups cubed, fully cooked ham
        (see "Stock Your Freezer:
        Bulk Recipes")
    1 can (10¾ ounces) cream of
        chicken soup
    1 cup (8 ounces) sour cream
    ½ cup chopped onion
    ½ cup sliced ripe olives, optional
    1 tablespoon prepared mustard
    ½ teaspoon seasoned salt
    1 teaspoon Worcestershire sauce

Topping

    1 cup soft breadcrumbs (or crushed
        crackers)
    2 tablespoons (¼ stick) cup butter or
        margarine, melted
    1 cup shredded cheese

Cook noodles for 10 minutes or until they just start to soften in boiling water; drain and place in a large bowl. Add the ham, soup, sour cream, onion, olives, mustard, seasoned salt, and Worcestershire sauce.

Transfer to 2 greased 9 x 13-inch baking dishes or foil pans. In a bowl, toss breadcrumbs and butter; add cheese. Sprinkle over casseroles. Cover one casserole with several layers of plastic wrap, label, and freeze.

Bake the second casserole, uncovered, at 325°F for 30 minutes or until heated through.

To Serve

Remove wrapping and bake frozen casserole, uncovered, at 350°F for 90 minutes. Or thaw in refrigerator overnight and bake, uncovered, at 325°F for 55 minutes or until heated through.

Kielbasa Sausage Stir-fry

Yield: 8 servings

1 green bell pepper, sliced in strips
1 carrot, julienned (cut in thin
    strips like matchsticks)
1 onion, thinly sliced
1 potato, julienned
2 large links frozen kielbasa sausage
1 tablespoon canola or vegetable oil
4 cups frozen cooked rice

Teriyaki Sauce
1 cup soy sauce
1 cup water
1 cup brown sugar, firmly packed
1 cup sugar
1 tablespoon minced ginger
1 green onion, chopped (optional)

Defrost kielbasa sausage, then slice it. Stir-fry all ingredients in a skillet on the stove until browned. Mix sauce and pour on top.

Bring to a boil and stir-fry for 5 minutes. Cool and freeze in two 8-inch square pans or in large zip-top bags.

To Serve
Thaw in microwave and serve hot over rice.

Sweet and Sour Pork

1 large can (20 ounces) pineapple
    tidbits
1 green pepper, diced
1 cup water
1 cup white vinegar
1½ pounds lean pork roast
⅓ cup soy sauce
½ cup sugar
4 tablespoons cornstarch
¾ cup cold water

Trim the fat from the pork roast and cube the meat. Brown the meat in a large skillet with a little oil in the pan. After pork is browned, place in slow cooker with the pineapple, green pepper, water, and vinegar. Cook on LOW for 6 hours.

Drain pork and reserve the liquid in a medium saucepan. Combine the cornstarch and cold water. When the liquid in the saucepan comes to a boil, add ⅓ cup soy sauce and ½ cup sugar. Add the cornstarch mixture and stir until thickened. Add more cornstarch mixed with cold water until sauce reaches desired thickness. Pour the sauce on the meat and serve over rice.

Jambalaya
Yield: 8 servings

> 1 pound kielbasa sausage, cut into ½-inch slices
> 1 pound boneless, skinless chicken breasts, cubed
> ½ pound uncooked medium shrimp, peeled and deveined (spicy garlic shrimp tastes best)
> 1 large onion, chopped
> ½ cup chopped green pepper
> 4 garlic cloves, minced
> 2 tablespoons butter
> 1 can (14½ ounces) diced tomatoes, undrained
> 1 can (6 ounces) tomato paste
> ½ teaspoon hot pepper sauce
> ¼ teaspoon cayenne pepper
> ¼ teaspoon garlic powder
> ½ teaspoon black pepper

In a large saucepan, sauté the sausage, chicken, onion, celery, green pepper, and garlic in butter until chicken is browned. Stir in the tomatoes, tomato paste, and seasonings. Bring to a boil, then reduce heat. Cover and simmer for 8 minutes or until chicken is no longer pink. Stir in shrimp, cover, and simmer for 4 minutes or until shrimp turn pink.

Serve over precooked frozen rice (see "Stock Your Freezer: Bulk Recipes"). Cool and freeze leftovers for 3 to 6 months in zip-top freezer bags.

To Serve
Defrost in the microwave and serve warm over hot rice.

Calzones
Yield: 8 calzones

> 2 pounds frozen bread dough
> 2 egg yolks (reserve egg whites)
> 2 tablespoons olive oil

1 cup grated Parmesan cheese, divided
(any cheese will work)
1 tablespoon oregano
pizza toppings

Break each frozen bread dough into 4 sections. Roll out each piece into a 7-inch circle. Mix together the egg yolks, olive oil, oregano, and ½ cup Parmesan cheese. Spread the egg mixture on the dough circles. Place toppings on the lower half of each dough circle, fold the top half over the toppings like a taco, and seal the calzone. Brush the top with egg whites or butter and sprinkle with remaining shredded Parmesan cheese.

Bake at 350°F for 20 minutes or until golden brown. Serve with pizza sauce. When they are cool, individually wrap any leftover calzones in plastic and freeze for later.

To Serve
Remove calzones from freezer as needed and discard plastic wrappings. Microwave on HIGH for 2 minutes, turning over after 1 minute. Top with heated pizza sauce.

Pizza Sauce
1 can (8 ounces) tomato sauce
1 tablespoon oregano
1 teaspoon minced garlic

Open can of sauce and add oregano and garlic. Stir carefully so that sauce will not spill. Freeze leftover sauce.

Pizza Stromboli
Yield: 2 pizza loaves

1 loaf (1 pound) frozen bread or pizza
dough, thawed
2 egg yolks (reserve egg whites)
1 tablespoon grated Parmesan cheese
1 tablespoon olive oil
½ tablespoon oregano
16 ounces sliced pepperoni
4 cups (16 ounces) shredded mozzarella
cheese
toppings (optional): mushrooms, diced
green pepper, olives, bacon bits,
browned Italian sausage, pineapple

On a greased countertop, roll out dough into a 10 x 15-inch rectangle. Pick up dough by folding it over your forearm, then place dough on a foil-lined cookie sheet.

In a bowl, combine egg yolks, Parmesan cheese, oil, and oregano. Brush on the dough. Sprinkle with pepperoni, cheese, etc. Roll up, jelly-roll style, starting with a long side, then pinch seam to seal and tuck ends under.

Turn roll so the seam side is down. With a knife, make slits every 2 inches along the top of the dough. Brush top with egg whites; sprinkle with sesame seeds.

Wrap one stromboli in plastic wrap, then label ("350°F, 35 minutes") and freeze. Bake the other stromboli at 350°F for 25 to 30 minutes or until golden brown. Warm pizza sauce, slice the stromboli, and serve.

To Serve

Bake at 350°F for 35 minutes and serve warm with pizza sauce. (Sauce can be frozen and placed next to the pizza loaf in the freezer.)

Green Chili Verde Sauce

Yield: 8 to 10 servings

1 onion, diced
1 green bell pepper, chopped
4 garlic cloves, chopped
1 tablespoon olive oil
1 small can (4 ounces) diced green chilies
7 tomatillos, finely chopped
2 pounds lean pork, trimmed and cubed
2 teaspoons oregano
½ teaspoon sage
1 teaspoon cumin
2 cups water
2 beef bouillon cubes
2 tablespoons cornstarch
1 tablespoon all-purpose flour
Salt and pepper to taste

Husk and wash tomatillos, then finely chop them. Trim fat from pork, then cut it into cubes. Sauté onion, green pepper, and garlic in olive oil over medium heat. Remove from heat. Place cubed pork into the same skillet and brown the meat.

Place the tomatillo mixture in a slow cooker. Add seasonings and browned pork. Cook on LOW for 2 to 8 hours, depending on how much time you have. (The longer this dish cooks, the more tender the meat will be and the better the sauce will taste.)

Serve warm on tortillas sprinkled with cheese and dollop of sour cream. As side dishes, serve Spanish rice, refried beans, and chips and salsa.

To Freeze

Cool green chili verde sauce and place in zip-top freezer bags. Lay flat to freeze. Defrost in microwave and serve warm over tortillas with cheese.

Seafood

Fish Tacos

Yield: 4 servings

½ cup fat-free mayonnaise
1 tablespoon lime juice
2 teaspoons milk
⅓ cup dry seasoned breadcrumbs
    (or season with garlic salt and
    parsley)
2 tablespoons lemon-pepper seasoning
1 egg, lightly beaten
1 teaspoon water
1 pound frozen orange roughy fillets,
    cut into 1-inch strips (any type
    of mild-tasting fish can be used)
4 six-inch corn tortillas, warmed
1 cup coleslaw mix or chopped lettuce
2 medium tomatoes, diced
1 cup shredded Mexican cheese blend
1 tablespoon minced fresh cilantro
pineapple salsa

In a small bowl, combine mayonnaise, lime juice, and milk; cover and refrigerate until serving time. In a shallow bowl, combine breadcrumbs and lemon pepper. In another shallow bowl, combine egg and water.

Defrost fish. Rinse and pat dry with paper towel. Dip fish in egg mixture, then roll in crumbs.

In a large nonstick skillet coated with cooking spray, cook fish over medium-high heat for 3 to 4 minutes on each side, or until it flakes easily with a fork.

Spoon on tortillas; top with tomatoes, cheese, cilantro, pineapple salsa, and coleslaw mix or lettuce.

Spicy Grilled Salmon

Yield: 8 servings

8 frozen salmon fillets
1 teaspoon olive oil
1 teaspoon salt

1 teaspoon cracked pepper
1 teaspoon garlic powder
½ teaspoon cayenne pepper
½ teaspoon paprika

Defrost the salmon. Mix the dry seasonings together in a large zip-top bag. Rub the salmon fillets with olive oil and then place them one at a time into the bag with the dry seasonings. Rub to coat with dry seasonings. Cook salmon fillets on a hot grill for 5 minutes on each side.

Shrimp and Biscuit Bake

Yield: two 9 x 13-inch pans (6 servings each)

½ cup oil
½ cup all-purpose flour
2 medium onions, finely chopped
2 cups chopped celery
4 bay leaves
2 teaspoons thyme
2 teaspoons lemon-pepper seasoning
3 teaspoons seasoned salt
2 cups chicken stock
2 cans (14½ ounces each) diced
    tomatoes
4 cups frozen deveined salad shrimp

Topping
2 eggs, beaten
⅔ cup milk
2 packages (12 ounces each) corn
    muffin mix

Heat the olive oil in a heavy pan, then add the flour and cook over medium to low heat until the mixture is quite dark in color. Add the onions and celery and cook until they begin to soften and become translucent. Then add the seasonings, stock, and tomatoes. Cover the pot and simmer on low heat for 30 minutes. Remove from heat and stir in the frozen shrimp. Divide the mixture into two 9 x 13-inch foil pans and let cool.

For the biscuit topping, mix together the eggs and milk, then add the muffin mix. Stir just until blended. Drop by tablespoonfuls on the shrimp mixture. Wrap both pans in layers of plastic wrap and label "400°F, 30 minutes."

To Serve
Preheat oven to 400°F. Remove wrappings from frozen casserole. Bake uncovered for 30 minutes or until biscuits are golden brown and casserole is warmed through.

Pasta Primavera with Shrimp and Sugar Snap Peas

Yield: two 9 x 13-inch pans (8 servings each)

1 package (12 ounces or about
   5 cups) uncooked egg noodles
3 tablespoons butter
2 pounds fresh sliced mushrooms
   (optional)
3 teaspoons fresh rosemary,
   chopped
3 teaspoons fresh minced or
   creamed garlic
salt and pepper to taste
1½ cup low-sodium chicken stock
1½ cup low-sodium beef stock
1 cup whipping cream
1½ pound frozen, deveined
   salad shrimp
2 cups chopped sugar snap peas
¼ cup grated Parmesan cheese
½ cup sliced almonds

Heat oven to 350°F and spray two 9 x 13 foil pans with cooking spray. In a large stockpot, cook pasta in boiling water for 12 minutes and drain.

Melt butter in a separate skillet. Add mushrooms and rosemary. Let cook for about 8 minutes without stirring, or until mushrooms are tender and golden brown. Flip over and cook for 2 minutes.

Add garlic and sauté until you can smell it. Add chicken and beef stocks to the pan. Bring to a boil and reduce liquid by half (about 10 minutes). Add whipping cream and reduce until thickened, about 8 minutes. Season to taste with salt and freshly ground pepper.

Remove from heat. In the large stockpot, mix the sauce with pasta, shrimp, and sugar snap peas. Divide mixture between two 9 x 13-inch foil pans. Top with grated Parmesan cheese and sliced almonds.

Wrap one pan of pasta primavera in plastic wrap and label ("350°F, 40 minutes if frozen, or 25 minutes if defrosted"). Bake the other pan, uncovered, for 25 minutes.

To Serve

Heat oven to 350°F and bake frozen dish, uncovered, for 40 minutes. Or defrost dish in the fridge overnight, then bake at 350°F for 25 minutes. Serve with a green salad and breadsticks.

Blackened Halibut

Yield: 4 servings

This dish contains previously frozen ingredients and should not be refrozen. Refrigerate leftovers and use within 4 days.

    2 pounds frozen halibut
    3 tablespoon Cajun seasoning

Defrost frozen fish in the microwave. Roll fish in Cajun seasoning and sear in a pan on medium-high heat. Cook fish for 4 minutes on each side or until it flakes with a fork. Serve immediately.

Grilled Fish

Yield: 8 servings

This dish contains previously frozen ingredients and should not be refrozen. Refrigerate leftovers use within 4 days.

    4 pounds frozen fish fillets (any variety)
    1 cup all-purpose flour
    1 tablespoon Italian seasoning

Flour both sides of fish fillets, season with salt and pepper, and sprinkle with Italian seasoning. Over medium-high heat, grill fish until it flakes with a fork, about 3 to 4 minutes each side. Serve with roasted vegetables.

Sweet & Spicy Plum Sauce

Yield: 1 cup (6 to 8 servings)

    ½ cup bottled plum sauce
    2 tablespoons lemon juice
    2 tablespoons sugar
    2 tablespoons soy sauce
    1 tablespoon chili powder or red pepper
        flakes
    2 tablespoons finely chopped fresh
        cilantro leaves (optional)

In a small bowl, mix all ingredients until smooth. Chill and serve over grilled fish.

Grilled Salmon

Yield: 4 servings

This dish contains previously frozen ingredients and should not be refrozen. Refrigerate leftovers and use within 4 days.

2 pounds frozen salmon fillets
½ cup vegetable oil
½ cup lemon juice
4 green onions, thinly sliced
3 tablespoons minced fresh parsley
1½ teaspoons minced fresh rosemary *or* ½
teaspoon dried rosemary
salt and pepper to taste

Defrost frozen salmon and place in a shallow dish. Combine remaining ingredients and mix well. Set aside ¼ cup for basting; pour rest over the salmon. Cover and refrigerate for 30 minutes. Drain and discard marinade.

Grill salmon over medium heat, skin side down, for 15 to 20 minutes or until fish flakes easily with a fork. Baste occasionally with reserved marinade.

Parmesan-Crusted Fish

Yield: 4 servings

2 pounds frozen or fresh fish (such as
halibut or cod)
1 cup large breadcrumbs (I prefer Panko
brand)
¼ cup Parmesan cheese
1 egg, beaten
½ cup all-purpose flour

Defrost fish. Mix together breadcrumbs and Parmesan cheese. Place flour, egg, and breadcrumb mixture in three shallow dishes.

Cover fish in flour, then dip in beaten egg, and then roll in breadcrumbs. Heat 1 tablespoon oil in a skillet. Fry fish for 4 minutes on each side. Serve hot.

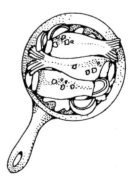

Vegetarian Dishes

Cashew Crunch

Yield: 8 servings

6 tablespoons soy sauce
¼ cup oyster sauce
4 teaspoons sesame oil
¼ cup water
1½ teaspoons sugar
¼ cup canola oil
2 carrots peeled, julienned
4 cups broccoli
1 package (14 ounces) extra-firm tofu, cut
    into cubes
4 garlic cloves, minced
3 teaspoons bottled minced ginger
1 cup roasted cashew nuts (add just before
    serving)
½ of 13.25-ounces package whole wheat
    rotini

Bring 5 cups water mixed with 1 tablespoon salt to a boil in a large stockpot. Pour in dry rotini and cook until pasta is al dente. Meanwhile, combine soy sauce, oyster sauce, sesame oil, water, and sugar in a small bowl. Heat 4 tablespoons canola oil in a large skillet. Stir-fry carrots and broccoli for 2 minutes. Add cubed tofu; stir-fry for 4 minutes. Add garlic and ginger and cook for 1 minute. Add sauce mixture and noodles. Stir to coat. Serve warm or place in plastic bags, label, and freeze.

To Serve
Heat cashew crunch in microwave, top with roasted cashews, and serve warm.

Orange Pecan Stir-fry

Yield: 8 servings

2 tablespoons olive oil
1 large package (32 ounces)
    frozen cauliflower, broccoli,
    and carrot mix
⅔ cup chopped pecans
½ cup frozen orange juice
6 cups cooked rice

Heat a skillet over high heat and add oil and vegetables. Stir-fry vegetables for 5 to 6 minutes or until they are tender. Stir in chopped pecans and orange juice concentrate. Serve over warmed rice.

Thai Lettuce Wraps

Yield: 8 servings

½ cup rice vinegar
½ cup canola oil
¼ cup lime juice
¼ cup mayonnaise
¼ cup creamy peanut butter
2 tablespoons brown sugar
2 tablespoons soy sauce
4 teaspoons minced fresh ginger
2 teaspoons sesame oil
2 teaspoons Thai chili sauce
2 garlic cloves, peeled
1 cup minced fresh cilantro,
    divided
1 package (16 ounces) firm tofu,
    drained and cut into ½-inch
    cubes
1 cup chopped green onions
1 cup shredded carrots
1 teaspoon crushed red pepper flakes
    (optional)
1 cup dry-roasted peanuts (reserve
    until ready to serve)
16 lettuce leaves

Place the first 11 ingredients in a blender; cover and process until smooth. Stir in ½ cup cilantro.

In a large bowl, combine the tofu, onions, carrots, and remaining ½ cup cilantro. Add dressing and toss to coat. Pour mixture into freezer bags, label, and freeze.

To Serve

Defrost tofu–cilantro dressing mixture in microwave and then divide among lettuce leaves. Add peanuts and scoop onto lettuce leaves. Top with ½ cup chopped dry-roasted peanuts.

Veggie Stuffed Shells

Yield: three 8-inch square pans (4 servings each)

1 package (12 ounces) jumbo pasta shells
½ pound (8 ounces) fresh
    mushrooms, chopped
1 medium onion, chopped
1 tablespoon olive oil
4 garlic cloves, minced
1 package (14 ounces) silken
    extra-firm tofu
3 tablespoons lime or lemon juice

1 package (10 ounces) frozen chopped
    spinach, thawed and squeezed dry
1 small can (2¼ ounces) sliced ripe black
    olives, drained
3 tablespoons minced fresh basil
1 tablespoon balsamic vinegar
salt and pepper to taste
6 cups or 2 jars (26 ounces each)
    meatless spaghetti sauce
1 tablespoon Italian seasoning
¼ cup pine nuts, chopped

Cook pasta according to package directions until al dente; drain. Meanwhile, in a large skillet, sauté mushrooms and onion in 1 tablespoon olive oil until tender. Add garlic; cook 1 minute longer.

In a large bowl, mash tofu with lemon juice. Stir in the spinach, olives, basil, salt, and pepper. Add to mushroom mixture; heat through. Spoon into shells.

Spread 1 cup spaghetti sauce in the bottom of each of two 8-inch square foil pans coated with cooking spray. Arrange shells over sauce; top with remaining sauce. Sprinkle with pine nuts. Cover, label ("375°F, 60 minutes"), and freeze.

To cook immediately, bake at 375°F for 30 minutes, then uncover and bake 5 to 10 minutes or until bubbly.

Mac 'n' Cheese

Yield: two 8-inch square pans (5 servings each)

1 package (16 ounces) whole-wheat elbow
    macaroni
½ cup diced onions (optional)
¼ cup (½ stick) butter
¼ cup all-purpose flour
3 teaspoons salt
1 tablespoon Worcestershire sauce
4¼ cups whole milk
3 cups shredded cheddar cheese

Topping

3 Roma tomatoes, diced
2 tablespoons butter
¾ cup large breadcrumbs (I use Panko
    brand)
1 cup crumbled bacon

Cook macaroni according to package directions for 6 to 7 minutes, or just until noodles are al dente (cooked but still chewy). Drain pasta. Rinse with cold water to stop the cooking process.

Heat butter in a saucepan over medium heat and sauté onion until translucent. Add flour; whisk until smooth. Add salt and Worcestershire sauce. Warm milk in microwave for 1 minute, then whisk it into the butter–flour mixture, stirring constantly until thickened. Turn off heat. Add cheddar cheese and stir until melted. Gently stir the macaroni into the cheese sauce. Add more salt and pepper to taste and then pour into two 8-inch square baking pans.

Cover top of mac 'n' cheese with diced tomatoes. Mix melted butter and breadcrumbs together and sprinkle over tomatoes. Spread crumbled bacon over top of breadcrumbs. Wrap in several layers of plastic wrap, label, and freeze.

To Serve

Thaw mac 'n' cheese for 48 hours in the refrigerator. Preheat oven to 350°F. Remove plastic wrap from mac 'n' cheese. Cover with foil and bake for 20 minutes (40 minutes if frozen). Remove cover and bake for 10 to 15 minutes or until golden brown and bubbly.

Tofu Manicotti

Yield: two 9 x 13-inch pans (8 servings each)

    4 cups spaghetti sauce
    2 cans (14½ ounces each) diced
        tomatoes, undrained
    1 cup shredded zucchini
    ½ cup shredded carrots
    2 teaspoons Italian seasoning
    2 packages (12 ounces) silken firm tofu
    1 small package (2 cups) cottage cheese
    2 cups (8 ounces) shredded mozzarella
        cheese
    2 tablespoons grated Parmesan cheese
    2 packages (8 ounces each) manicotti

Combine the spaghetti sauce, tomatoes, zucchini, carrots, and Italian seasoning. Spread ¾ cup of sauce mixture into each of two 9 x 13-inch foil pans coated with cooking spray.

Combine the tofu and cheeses; stuff into uncooked manicotti shells. Place over spaghetti sauce; top with remaining sauce. Pour ¼ inch water around the edge of each pan and wrap each pan in several layers of plastic wrap. Label and freeze.

To Serve

If defrosted, cover and bake at 375°F for 50 to 55 minutes, or until noodles are tender. If frozen, double the cooking time. Let stand for 5 minutes before serving.

School Lunches

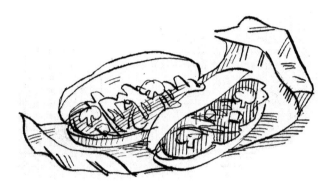

Mini Calzones

Yield: 8 calzones

> 1 pound frozen bread dough
> 1 egg yolk
> 1 tablespoon olive oil
> 1 tablespoon grated Parmesan cheese
>   (any cheese will work)
> ½ tablespoon dried oregano
> pizza toppings

Defrost frozen bread dough for 10 seconds in the microwave. Slice frozen bread dough into 4 sections and then cut each section in half to create 8 sections of dough. Roll out each piece into a 4- to 5-inch circle.

Mix egg yolk, oil, oregano, and cheese, then spread on dough. Place toppings on half of each dough circle, then fold over other half of circle and seal. Brush top with egg whites or butter and sprinkle with shredded Parmesan cheese.

Bake at 350°F for 15 to 20 minutes or until golden brown. Individually wrap leftover calzones in plastic and freeze.

To Serve

Take calzones out of the freezer as needed. Remove plastic and heat calzones, one at a time, in the microwave for 2 minutes, turning over after 1 minute. Top with warm pizza sauce.

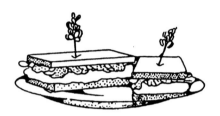

Tuna Fish Sandwiches

Yield: 8 to 10 servings

> 1 package (8 ounces) cream cheese,
>   softened
> ¼ cup salad dressing, such as Miracle
>   Whip
> 2 cans (6 ounces each) chunk tuna,
>   drained
> ½ cup chopped green onion
> ½ cup chopped cashew nuts
> ½ cup shredded carrots
> 2 tablespoons lemon juice
> 16 slices whole-wheat bread

In a medium bowl, combine cream cheese and salad dressing and beat until smooth. Stir in tuna, onions, carrot, cashew nuts, and lemon juice.

Spread tuna filling on slices of bread to make sandwiches. Slice each sandwich in half and wrap each half individually in plastic wrap and place in a large freezer bag. Label the bag of sandwiches and freeze.

To Serve

Let sandwiches defrost overnight in the refrigerator, or add to lunchboxes in the morning and let thaw until lunchtime. Make sure sandwiches are eaten within 2 hours of thawing completely.

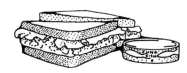

Chicken Pesto Sandwiches

Yield: 5 servings

1 package (8 ounces) cream cheese, softened
¼ cup ranch salad dressing
⅓ cup spinach pesto (see recipe below or use store-bought pesto) or salsa
1½ cups chopped cooked chicken
10 slices whole-wheat bread

In medium bowl, combine cream cheese and ranch dressing; beat until smooth. Stir in pesto and cheeses, then add chicken.

Spread chicken filling on bread to make sandwiches. Wrap each sandwich individually in plastic wrap and place in a large freezer bag. Label the bag of sandwiches and freeze.

To Serve

Let sandwiches defrost overnight in refrigerator, or add to lunchboxes in the morning and let thaw until lunchtime. Make sure sandwiches are eaten within 2 hours of thawing completely.

Spinach Pesto

2 cups fresh spinach leaves, washed and stemmed
½ cup fresh parsley
½ cup walnuts or pine nuts, toasted
¼ cup Parmesan cheese, freshly grated, not canned
3 garlic cloves
2 tablespoons extra-virgin olive oil
¼ teaspoon salt
⅛ teaspoon pepper

Place all ingredients in food processor and process to a fine paste. Taste pesto and adjust seasonings to taste.

Transfer pesto to a glass container and top with a thin coat of olive oil to prevent the top of the pesto from discoloring.

This pesto keeps for weeks in the refrigerator or can be frozen.

Homemade Corn Dogs
Yield: 16 servings

    1½ cups cornmeal
    1½ cups all-purpose flour
    2 teaspoons baking powder
    ½ teaspoon salt
    2 eggs, beaten
    2 cups milk
    2 packages (8 in each) hotdogs
    16 wooden skewers
    Oil for deep-fat frying

Combine cornmeal, flour, salt, and baking powder, then add the eggs and mix well. Stir in milk to make a thick batter; pour into a tall glass and let stand a few minutes. Pat hotdogs dry and insert sticks. In a large pot, heat oil to 375°F. Dip each hotdog in the batter and then carefully place it in the hot oil. Flip using hotdog tongs. Fry until golden brown and then set on a paper towel.

After corn dogs have cooled, wrap each individually in plastic wrap and place in a large freezer bag. Label and freeze.

To Serve
Let corn dogs defrost overnight in refrigerator, or add to lunchboxes in the morning and let thaw until lunchtime.

Taco Pita Sandwiches
Yield: 16 sandwiches

    1 cup frozen browned taco beef, thawed
    2 cups refried beans
    1 cup salsa
    1 can (14½ ounces) kidney beans, rinsed
        and drained
    1½ cups shredded cheese
    8 whole-wheat pita pockets, halved

In medium bowl, combine taco meat, refried beans, and salsa; mix well. Stir in kidney beans and cheese. Spoon mixture into pita pockets and individually wrap each sandwich, then label and freeze. Place in insulated lunchboxes with gel packs and let thaw until lunchtime. You can pack a small bag of shredded lettuce for your child to add to the sandwich if you think he or she will eat it.

Chewy Granola Bars

Yield: two 9 x 13-inch pans (about 16 bars each)

Crust

>   2 cups all-purpose flour
>   ⅔ cup brown sugar, firmly packed
>   ½ cup finely chopped walnuts
>   ⅔ cup (1 stick plus 3 tablespoons)
>   butter, melted

Filling

>   4 eggs
>   ½ cup sugar
>   1½ cups brown sugar, firmly packed
>   4 teaspoons vanilla
>   2 tablespoons all-purpose flour
>   1 teaspoon baking powder
>   ½ teaspoon salt
>   1½ cups chopped dried berries
>   2 cups chopped walnuts or pecans
>   1 cup shredded coconut
>   1⅓ cup granola or quick-cooking oats
>   powdered sugar

Preheat oven to 350°F. For crust, mix together 2 cups flour, ⅔ cup brown sugar, and ½ cup walnuts; blend in melted butter until crumbs form. Press into 2 greased (or foil) 9 x 13-inch pans. Bake at 350°F for 10 minutes until light golden brown.

Meanwhile, in a large bowl, beat eggs until fluffy. Gradually add ½ cup sugar and 1½ cup brown sugar. Then stir in vanilla. Add flour, baking powder, and salt. Then add dried berries, nuts, coconut, and granola. Pour over partially baked crust and bake for 20 to 25 minutes longer, or until bars are set. Cool for about 1 hour, then cut into bars and roll in powdered sugar. Slice and place in zip-top freezer bags, or wrap bars individually for a quick lunchbox treat.

Peanut Butter Granola Wraps

Yield: 12 servings

>   1½ cups peanut butter
>   1½ cups granola
>   ½ cup chopped peanuts
>   3 tablespoons honey
>   8 medium (10-inch) whole-wheat
>   tortillas

In a large bowl, combine peanut butter, granola, chopped peanuts, and honey; mix well. Spread tortillas with the peanut butter mixture so they are completely covered and the mixture is ¼ inch thick. Roll up tortillas and cut in half. Serve immediately, or wrap well and freeze. Let thaw in an insulated lunchbox until lunchtime.

Pizza Muffins

Yield: 20 muffins

2½ cups all-purpose flour
2 teaspoons baking powder
½ teaspoon baking soda
½ teaspoon salt
1 teaspoon garlic powder
1 teaspoon dried basil leaves
½ teaspoon dried oregano
1 tablespoon sugar
1 cup diced pepperoni
2 cups shredded sharp cheddar cheese,
    divided
4 green onions, chopped
1 egg, beaten
1½ cups buttermilk

Preheat oven to 375°F. Line 2 cupcake pans with paper muffin liners. In a large bowl, mix together flour, baking powder, baking soda, salt, basil, oregano, and sugar. Mix in green onions and 1 cup cheese.

In a smaller bowl beat the egg, then whisk in buttermilk. Add the buttermilk mixture to the flour mixture and stir to combine thoroughly. Spoon batter into paper-lined muffin cups until half full. Sprinkle remaining 1 cup cheese on top of muffins.

Bake at 375°F for 15 minutes, or until a toothpick inserted into center of the muffin comes out clean.

To make jumbo pizza muffins, use a jumbo muffin tin (sprayed with cooking spray) and increase the cooking time by a few minutes. Watch closely to make sure muffins don't overcook and dry out. Insert a toothpick to check doneness.

Cool muffins, individually wrap in plastic, and freeze in a large zip-top bag. Place one or two muffins in a lunchbox and they will defrost and be ready to eat by lunch time.

Mini Pizzas

Yield: 24 pizzas

12 English muffins
1 can (8 ounces) tomato sauce
1 tablespoon oregano
1 teaspoon minced garlic
24 slices pepperoni (or Canadian bacon)
4 cups shredded cheese

Preheat oven to 350°F. Slice open the English muffins, then butter and toast them in the oven on a baking sheet for 4 minutes. Olive oil can be used in place of butter.

As soon as the English muffins come out of the oven, top them with shredded cheese. This will seal the muffins so the pizza sauce will not make them soggy.

Mix together the tomato sauce, oregano, and garlic. Spoon a small amount of sauce on each muffin, then top with more shredded cheese and pepperoni slices. (I like to dice my pepperoni if I have extra time, so all the toppings don't come off in one bite.)

Place mini pizzas back in the oven on a foil-covered baking sheet for 5 to 6 minutes or until cheese is completely melted. Cool the pan and place it in the freezer for 1 hour.

When pizzas are frozen, individually wrap them and place them in a large zip-top bag. In the morning, add a mini pizza or two to lunchboxes and let them thaw until lunchtime.

Soups, Salads, and Sides

Soups

Minestrone Soup

Yield: 10 servings

8 cups water
2 cans (14½ ounces each) diced tomatoes
1 can (14½ ounces) kidney or navy beans
1 can (14½ ounces) green beans
1 can (14½ ounces) corn
1 medium onion, chopped
2 carrots, thinly sliced
4 ounces Polish sausage, sliced
2 tablespoons parsley
1 bay leaf
2 teaspoons salt
¼ teaspoon pepper
4 ounces wide egg noodles, uncooked

Place all ingredients except noodles in a large stockpot and bring to a boil. Simmer for 20 minutes, then cool and place in zip-top bags. Label and freeze.

To Serve
Defrost soup in microwave while you bring 4 cups of water to a boil. Cook noodles in the boiling water until al dente. Drain and mix into the warm soup. Serve soup hot with crackers or toasted bread.

Ham and Broccoli Cheese Soup

Yield: 7 servings

2 cups cubed potatoes
1½ cups water
1½ cups cubed, fully cooked ham
1 onion, chopped
3 tablespoons butter or margarine
3 tablespoons all-purpose flour
¼ teaspoon pepper
3 cups milk
1½ cups (6 ounces) finely shredded
  cheddar cheese
1 cup frozen broccoli florets, thawed and
  chopped

In a saucepan, bring potatoes and water to a boil. Cover and cook for 10 to 15 minutes or until tender. Drain, reserving 1 cup cooking liquid; set potatoes and liquid aside. In a large saucepan, sauté ham and onion in butter until onion is tender.

Stir in the flour and pepper until smooth; gradually add milk and reserved cooking liquid. Bring to a boil; cook and stir for 2 minutes or until thickened. Reduce heat to low.

Add the cheese, broccoli, and reserved potatoes; cook and stir until cheese is melted and soup is heated through. Freeze in zip-top bags and label.

To Serve

Defrost soup in the microwave on HIGH for 6 minutes or until warmed through. Serve hot with cornbread.

Vegetable Beef Stew

Yield: 10 to 15 servings

5 to 6 medium potatoes, cubed
1 pound cooked beef, shredded
3 carrots, sliced
1 onion, chopped
1 stalk celery, chopped
3 to 4 cups chicken stock
2 teaspoons dried thyme
1 teaspoon dried parsley
1 cup rice, uncooked
1 can (14½ ounces) green beans
1 can (14½ ounces) corn
1 can (14½ ounces) navy beans
1 can (14½ ounces) diced tomatoes
1 large can (29 ounces) tomato sauce
2 cups water

Combine all ingredients except for green beans, navy beans, corn, tomato sauce, and water in a 5-quart slow cooker. Cover and cook on HIGH for 2 hours.

Purée one cup of the mixture and add back to slow cooker to thicken the soup. Stir in green beans, navy beans, corn, tomato sauce, and water. Cover and cook on HIGH for 1 hour, then reduce to LOW and cook for 6 hours.

Cool soup and freeze in zip-top bags. Don't forget to label the bags.

To Serve

Defrost soup in the microwave on HIGH for 6 minutes and serve hot with crackers or toasted bread.

Chicken Noodle Soup

Yield: 8 to 10 servings

    4 cups chicken stock
    6 cups water
    2 cups frozen diced vegetables (peas,
        carrots, corn, etc.)
    1 pound cooked chicken or turkey,
        chopped or shredded
    1½ teaspoons Italian seasoning
    1 teaspoon salt
    2 packages country gravy mix
    1½ cups egg noodles (reserve until serving
        time)

Mix together chicken stock, vegetables, chicken, and seasonings. Bring to a boil for 6 to 7 minutes. Add gravy mix and simmer for 10 minutes.

Let the soup cool, then freeze it in double-layered zip-top bags. To serve the soup right away, add the noodles and boil for 8 to 10 minutes.

To Serve

Remove the plastic bags and place the frozen soup in a glass bowl. Defrost soup in the microwave on HIGH until hot. Meanwhile, bring water to a boil and add uncooked egg noodles. Boil until noodles are al dente, then mix into the soup. Serve soup hot with salty crackers.

Hearty Beef and Bean Soup

Yield: 10 servings

    3 tablespoons olive oil
    1 red onion, chopped
    2 garlic cloves, minced
    1 extra-large can (29 ounces) tomato sauce
    6 cups water
    ½ tablespoon dried parsley
    ½ tablespoon dried basil
    ½ tablespoon dried oregano
    2 teaspoons garlic salt
    3 bay leaves
    1 can (14½ ounces) navy or great
        northern beans
    1 can (15 ounces) chili with beef
        (or another can of beans and 1 pound
        browned ground beef)
    1 can (14½ ounces) corn
    salt and pepper to taste

In a large pot over medium heat, cook onion in olive oil until translucent. Stir in garlic and cook until tender. Stir in remaining ingredients. Bring to a boil and then simmer for 10 minutes.

Cool and place in freezer bags. Label and freeze up to 2 months.

To Serve

Defrost soup in microwave on HIGH for 6 minutes and serve with warm garlic bread or crackers.

Taco Soup

Yield: 10 servings

> 1 pound frozen cooked ground beef,
>   thawed
> 1 medium onion, chopped
> 1 package taco seasoning mix
>   (or 3 tablespoons taco seasoning)
> 1 can (14½ ounces) corn, drained
> 1 can (14½ ounces) black beans,
>   drained (kidney or navy beans will
>   work too)

> 1 large can (28 ounces) sliced stewed
>   tomatoes, drained
> 1 can (8 ounces) tomato sauce

Sauté chopped onion in a large stockpot with precooked ground beef. Stir in taco seasoning and remaining ingredients. Bring to a boil and then lower heat and simmer for 20 minutes.

Cool and place in freezer zip-top bags and label. Double-bag soup to prevent spills.

To Serve

Defrost soup in microwave and serve with chips, grated cheese, and sour cream.

Cheesy Hamburger Soup

Yield: 8 to 10 servings

> 1 pound ground beef, browned
> 1 cup diced onion
> 1 cup diced celery
> 3 cups water
> 3 cubes beef bouillon
> 4 cups diced potatoes
> 2 large carrots, shredded
> 4 tablespoons (½ stick) butter, melted
> ¼ cup all-purpose flour

2 cups shredded cheddar cheese
1½ cups milk
1 teaspoon dried basil
1 teaspoon dried parsley flakes
salt and pepper to taste

Sauté the onion and celery with 1 tablespoon olive oil in a large pot until the onions have softened. Add browned ground beef, water, and beef bouillon cubes. Bring water to a boil. Add potatoes and carrots and boil for 10 minutes.

In a small saucepan, stir together butter and flour. Mix until smooth and add milk. Stir until thickened and shredded cheddar cheese. Stir until cheese is melted. Pour the cheese mixture into the large pot of boiling water with vegetables. Add basil and parsley, then warm up. Salt and pepper to taste.

Serve hot or freeze when the soup has cooled. Pour the soup into doubled zip-top bags, then label and freeze flat.

To Serve
Simply defrost soup on the microwave on HIGH until it is warmed all the way through.

Mini Meatball Soup
Yield: 6 servings

1 quart (4 cups) chicken broth
1 pound ground turkey (or ground chicken or beef)
1 carrot, peeled and grated
½ small onion, grated
1 garlic clove, grated
3 tablespoons shredded Parmesan cheese
3 tablespoons dry breadcrumbs
3 teaspoons parsley
salt and pepper to taste
1 large box (12 ounces) uncooked rotini (or any type of small, sturdy pasta)

In a medium-size pot, cook pasta according to directions on bag until it is al dente. In a separate large pot, bring the chicken broth to a boil and then simmer.

In a zip-top bag, combine remaining ingredients. Cut off about ½ inch at one of the corners, then squeeze the mixture through the tip. Cut off the meat mixture every ½ inch or so with a pair of kitchen scissors and let drop into the pot.

Simmer the mini meatballs in the chicken broth for 6 to 7 minutes or until fully cooked. Drain the rotini and add to the chicken broth and meatballs. Label and freeze soup in zip-top plastic bags.

To Serve

Defrost soup the in microwave and serve hot with crackers or toasted bread.

Black Bean Soup

Yield: 10 servings

1 bag (16 ounces) dried black beans
1 can (14½ ounces) corn
1 cup dried onion flakes (or 1 medium onion, minced)
2 tablespoons garlic powder
2 tablespoons cumin
3 chicken bouillon cubes
salt and pepper to taste
fresh cilantro

Place black beans in a slow cooker and add enough water to cover them. Cook all night on LOW. In the morning, scoop out all but 2 cups of beans and place in zip-top bags to freeze and use later.

To the remaining bean liquid and 2 cups of beans, add the corn, onion, garlic powder, cumin, salt, pepper, and chicken bouillon cubes. Smash the beans with a potato masher and let the soup heat on LOW for about 20 minutes. Serve in a bowl with shredded cheese and tortilla chips.

French Onion Soup

Yield: 6 to 8 servings

4 large onions
5 tablespoons olive oil
½ cup dry sherry (optional)
2 bay leaves
1 bundle fresh thyme sprigs
1 quart chicken stock

Place onions in the freezer for 15 minutes before slicing so they won't sting your eyes. Slice onions and stir into a large pot with olive oil. Sprinkle with salt and cover the pot, then cook for 20 minutes. Uncover and cook for 1 hour on low heat. (This is necessary to get the caramelized onions you need for a good French onion soup.)

After 1 hour, add the sherry and let the liquid reduce by half. Add the bay leaves, fresh thyme, and chicken stock. Let the soup simmer for another hour. If necessary, add more water and salt to get the desired consistency and taste.

When soup has cooled completely, pour into zip-top bags, label, and freeze.

To Serve

Defrost frozen soup in the microwave and serve with toasted cheese bread.

Clam Chowder

Yield: 8 to 10 servings

2 cans (4½ ounces each) minced clams
½ cup chopped cooked bacon
1 medium onion, diced
2 stalks celery, diced

2 cups red potatoes, diced
¾ cup (1½ sticks) butter
¾ cup all-purpose flour
1 quart whipping cream
1 cup milk
salt and pepper to taste
1 teaspoon dried thyme
1 teaspoon dried basil
½ teaspoon sugar

Dice onions, celery, and potatoes; sauté with chopped bacon in a large pot until onions are tender. Drain clams and add them with 2 cups of water to the pot. Bring to a boil and simmer 15 to 20 minutes.

In a separate medium saucepan, melt the butter and add the flour. Stir together until smooth. Add the whipping cream and milk and simmer for 10 minutes. Pour on top of the vegetables in the pot and add seasonings. Cool soup and pour into large zip-top bags. Label and freeze.

To Serve

Defrost clam chowder in the microwave on HIGH until heated through. (Be sure to use a microwave-safe dish.) Serve warm in bread bowls or with crackers.

Salads and Sides

Chilled Broccoli and Bacon Salad

Yield: 6 servings

2 pounds frozen broccoli
4 to 5 strips frozen cooked bacon, thawed and crumbled (see "Stock Your Freezer: Bulk Recipes")
1 cup salad dressing (I use Miracle Whip)
¼ cup sugar
2 tablespoons vinegar (red wine or white)

Defrost broccoli in the microwave until warm. Stir remaining ingredients together and add broccoli. Stir until broccoli is covered, then chill and serve.

This salad does not freeze well once mixed together. Refrigerate leftovers and use within 3 to 4 days.

Snickers Salad

Yield: 8 to 10 servings)

4 Snickers candy bars (2.07 ounces each), cut into ½-inch chunks
5 medium tart apples, peeled and chopped
1 small container (8 ounces) frozen whipped topping, thawed
3 drops food coloring (your choice)

Unwrap and slice Snickers candy bars into ½-inch chunks. Peel and chop the apples. Mix together candy bars and apple chunks in a bowl.

In a separate bowl, mix together food coloring and whipped topping. Add to apples and candy bar chunks and stir until all pieces are completely covered with whipped topping. Pour into a large zip-top bag, label, and freeze until ready to serve.

To Serve

Remove the salad from the freezer 1 to 2 hours before you are ready to serve it. Set it in a large bowl and let it defrost on the counter. Serve the salad cold as a side dish.

Berry Fruit Salad

Yield: 10 servings

1½ cups (12 ounces) cottage cheese
1 small container (8 ounces) frozen
    whipped topping
1 small box (3 ounces) raspberry or
    strawberry gelatin mix
1 pound frozen mixed berries

Defrost the whipped topping for 20 seconds in the microwave.

Stir all ingredients together and serve chilled.

Potato Skins

Yield: 8 servings

8 large potatoes (1 per person)
2 cups cheddar cheese
⅓ cup sour cream
1 tablespoon snipped fresh chives
1½ cups crumbled cooked bacon
1 green onion chopped

Preheat oven to 350°F. Clean the potatoes with a soft bristle brush and then dry them. Poke potatoes all over with a fork (6 to 12 stabs). Drizzle olive oil over potatoes and place them in the oven on a baking sheet. Bake potatoes until done (about an hour, depending on size of potato).

When potatoes are fully cooked, cut them in half. Scrape out middle with spoon, leaving some potato on the skins. Heat 2 cups canola oil on high heat in a large pot on the stove. Drop in potato skins and deep-fry until golden brown. Drain on paper towels.

Once all potato skins have been fried, cover them with crumbled bacon, shredded cheese, and green onion slices. Place potato skins on a cookie sheet and freeze for 1 hour, then put them in a zip-top bag and freeze for up to 2 months.

To Serve

Preheat oven at 350°F. Take out frozen potato skins and place on a foil-covered baking sheet in the oven until the cheese melts. Mix together the sour-cream dipping sauce (recipe follows), and serve the potato skins warm with the dipping sauce.

Sour-Cream Dipping Sauce

Yield: 1 cup (4 servings)

1 cup sour cream
3 tablespoons fresh snipped chives

Mix together the sour cream and chives. Place in a covered container in the refrigerator until potato skins are ready to serve.

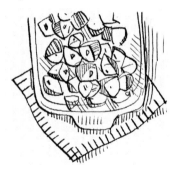

Cheesy Potatoes

Yield: two 9 x 13-inch pans (8 to 10 servings each)

2 large bags (32 ounces each) frozen
    shredded hash browns*
4 cans (10¾ ounces each) cream of
    chicken soup
4 cups sour cream
3 cups shredded cheddar cheese
1 cup (2 sticks) butter or
    margarine, melted

1 large onion, diced
2 teaspoons salt (add more to taste)
1 tablespoon garlic powder
2 teaspoons cracked pepper
4 cups finely crushed cornflakes
    or buttery crackers
¼ cup (½ stick) butter or margarine,
    melted

In an extra-large bowl, combine soups, sour cream, cheese, onions, and 1 cup melted butter. Stir in the hash browns and then divide mixture between two 9 x 13-inch pans.

Combine crushed cornflakes (or crackers) and ¼ cup melted butter ; sprinkle on top of both pans. Wrap in layers of plastic wrap and then label and freeze.

To Serve

Preheat oven to 350°F. Remove the wrappings from 1 pan of frozen cheesy potatoes. Bake for 1 hour or until the sauce is warm all the way through. This is a perfect side dish for a ham dinner.

*Cubed potatoes or thinly sliced potatoes may be used instead of hash browns, but they will need to be boiled (to soften them) before they are added to the sauce mixture.

Guacamole

Yield: 4 cups (8 servings)

8 ripe avocados
6 limes, juiced
1 red onion, chopped
2 garlic cloves, minced
2 large handfuls fresh cilantro, finely
    chopped
olive oil
salt and pepper

Halve and pit the avocados. Scoop out avocado flesh with a large spoon into a mixing bowl. Mash avocados with a fork, leaving them somewhat chunky. Add the remaining ingredients and mix together. So that it doesn't brown, immediately place the guacamole into 2 zip-top bags. Then label and freeze.

To Serve

Defrost frozen guacamole in the refrigerator overnight or in the microwave until all the ice crystals are gone. Serve chilled.

Seven-Layer Dip

Yield: two 8-inch square pans (8 servings each)

3 pounds ground beef
2 cans (14½ ounces each) refried beans
8 cups shredded cheddar–Monterey Jack
    cheese blend
1 large container (16 ounces) sour cream
2 cups guacamole
2 cups salsa
2 small cans (2.25 ounces each) chopped
    black olives
1 cup chopped tomatoes
1 cup chopped green onions

In a large skillet, brown ground beef. Set aside to drain and cool to room temperature.

Spread the beans into the bottom of two 9 x 13-inch pans that are lined with foil. Sprinkle 2 cups shredded cheese on top of beans. Sprinkle browned beef on top of the cheese. Carefully spread sour cream on top of beef. Spread guacamole on top of sour cream. Pour salsa over guacamole and spread evenly. Sprinkle with remaining shredded cheese. Sprinkle black olives, tomatoes, and green onions on top.

Wrap pans in layers of plastic, label, and freeze.

To Serve

Let dip defrost in the refrigerator overnight or on the countertop for an hour. This dip is best served cold with chips.

Tomato Salsa

Yield: 14 cups salsa

  5 medium green peppers
  1 jalapeno pepper, diced (add more for
      more heat)
  1 large white onion
  10 large tomatoes
  2½ tablespoons garlic-spread seasoning
  4 beef bouillon cubes
  1 heaping tablespoon sugar
  1 cup white vinegar

Wash and the seed peppers and core the tomatoes. In a large pot, combine vinegar and seasonings; bring to a boil over medium heat.

In a food processor, purée peppers, onion, and tomatoes. Pour into the large pot. Stir together and cook until salsa thickens.

Cool and pour into freezer zip-top bags. Label and freeze up to 6 months.

To Serve

Defrost frozen salsa in the microwave and pour off the extra water. Serve chilled with chips.

Pineapple Salsa

Yield 4 cups salsa

  4 cups diced fresh pineapple
  4 medium tomatoes, seeded and diced
  1½ cups diced red onion
  1½ cups minced fresh cilantro
  2 jalapeno peppers, seeded and diced
      (or 3 teaspoons crushed red pepper
      flakes)
  2 tablespoons olive oil
  2 teaspoons ground coriander
  1½ teaspoons ground cumin
  1 teaspoon salt
  1 teaspoon minced garlic
  1 tablespoon lime zest (grated peel)

Mix all ingredients together in a bowl. (I dice the first 4 ingredients, then put the remaining ingredients in a food processor so the cilantro is minced.) Pour into sandwich-size zip-top bags and freeze.

Defrost overnight in the refrigerator, or in the microwave for 3 to 4 minutes. Serve cold on fish tacos or with chips.

Spanish Rice
Yield: 6 servings

   3 cups long-grain white rice
   2 cans (14½ ounces each) diced tomatoes
   2 cans (4 ounces each) diced green chilies
   4 tablespoons taco seasoning
   6 ⅔ cups water

Combine all ingredients in a large pot and bring to boil. Reduce heat to medium-low and simmer, covered, for 20 to 30 minutes. Remove from heat. Let stand covered for 5 minutes. Fluff with a fork and serve or let cool. Once the rice has cooled, place in zip-top bags, label, and freeze.

To Serve
Place frozen rice in the microwave and heat on HIGH for 4 to 5 minutes. Rice should be fluffy and moist.

Holiday Cheese Balls
Yield: 2 cheese balls

   4 packages (8 ounces) cream
       cheese
   2 small cans (8½ ounces each)
       crushed pineapple, drained
       until dry
   ¼ cup minced onion
   ½ cup chopped green pepper
   4 cups chopped pecans or walnuts,
       divided
   2 tablespoons seasoned salt
   2 maraschino cherries

Mix together the cream cheese, crushed pineapple, minced onion, green pepper, and 2 cups chopped nuts. Roll the mixture into 2 balls and wrap in layers of plastic wrap. Place cheese balls in a zip-top bag and freeze.

To Serve
Remove the wrappings from the cheese balls 30 minutes before serving. Crush the reserved 2 cups nuts; roll the cheese balls in the crushed nuts. Decorate with parsley and a place a maraschino cherry on top.

Barbecued Beans

Yield: 16 servings

4 slices bacon, chopped
½ medium onion, diced
1 tablespoon fresh chopped rosemary
1 large can (28 ounces) baked beans
¼ cup brown sugar, firmly packed
½ cup barbecue sauce
salt and pepper

Chop and brown the bacon in a large saucepan until crisp. Add the diced onions and rosemary to the crisped bacon and sauté for 2 minutes. Add the beans, brown sugar, barbecue sauce, and salt and pepper to taste.

Serve warm or place in zip-top freezer bags. Label "barbecue beans" and freeze.

To Serve
Defrost beans and warm in the microwave. Top with fresh chopped rosemary and serve warm.

Egg Rolls

Yield: 10 servings

2 tablespoons olive oil
1 large bok choy cabbage, finely chopped (about 6 cups)
6 green onions, chopped
2 tablespoons soy sauce
2 teaspoons brown sugar
1 pound ground pork (ground turkey or beef may be substituted)
1 package egg-roll wrappers (4½-inch x 5½-inch)
4 cups canola or vegetable oil

In a large skillet over medium-high heat, stir-fry the ground pork until it is no longer pink. Slice the bok choy in half and then, moving from the inside out, thinly slice the cabbage into long strips. Discard the root. In a large bowl, mix together the cooked ground pork, sliced cabbage, and green onions.

Stir-fry the cabbage and green onions for 3 minutes in 2 tablespoons olive oil. Then add soy sauce, brown sugar, and ground pork. Stir-fry for 1 minute and then drain and cool.

Heat 4 cups oil in a large pot on medium-high heat before wrapping the egg rolls.

To wrap, lay the egg-roll wrapper out with the short (4½-inch) side directly in front of you. This will be the dry side. Place 1 tablespoon filling in the middle of the wrapper, spreading it out but not getting too close to the edges. Wet your fingertip and spread a bit of water along the wrapper edges. Tuck in the edges of the short sides and wrap the long side over, then roll like a burrito. Press down firmly on all sides to make sure they are well sealed.

When oil is ready, slide each egg roll carefully into the pot one at a time. Deep-fry until egg rolls are golden brown, then drain on paper towels. Place egg rolls on a baking sheet and freeze for 1 hour. Then place egg rolls in a zip-top bag to use later.

To Serve

Place frozen egg rolls on a foil-covered baking sheet in the oven at 425°F for 15 to 20 minutes, or until they are warmed through and crunchy. Serve with sweet-and-sour dipping sauce (recipe follows).

Sweet and Sour Dipping Sauce

Yield: 2 cups sauce (6 to 8 servings)

1 cup brown sugar, firmly packed
1½ tablespoons cornstarch
1 cup chicken broth
⅔ cup red wine vinegar
½ green pepper, minced
¼ cup corn syrup
¼ cup soy sauce
3 teaspoons minced ginger
2 teaspoons minced garlic

In a saucepan, combine the brown sugar and the cornstarch. Add the remaining ingredients and stir until thick and bubbly. Cook an additional 2 minutes and serve warm with egg rolls.

Ham Fried Rice

Yield: 6 servings

2 large eggs, lightly beaten
3½ to 4 tablespoons canola oil
3½ cups cold cooked rice
½ cup crumbled cooked bacon
½ cup frozen peas
3 tablespoons chopped green onions
1 teaspoon salt
1 tablespoon soy sauce

Heat a wok or a small, heavy skillet over high heat. Add 1½ tablespoons oil and swirl to coat the pan. When the pan is very hot, add the eggs and scramble them. Remove them from the pan before they brown. They should be soft and a bit runny.

Heat skillet again and add 2 tablespoons oil. Add the rice and toss to coat (about 2 to 3 minutes). Add the crumbled bacon and peas. Toss the ingredients until they are heated through (about 30 seconds). Add soy sauce and scrambled eggs; toss to combine. Season with salt. Garnish with chopped green onions.

When fried rice has cooled, place it in sandwich-size zip-top bags, then label and freeze.

To Serve

Defrost in microwave in the zip-top bag (it will act as a steamer) until warmed through (4 to 5 minutes), then serve.

Homemade Freezer Jam

Yield: 7 cups jam

> 3¼ cups frozen raspberries
> ¼ cup lemon juice
> 1 cup light corn syrup
> 1 package (2 ounces) pectin
> 4½ cups sugar

Using a potato masher, crush raspberries 1 cup at a time. (Do not purée.) When all raspberries are crushed, mix in ¼ cup lemon juice to preserve the color of the fruit. Stir in 1 box pectin, stirring every 5 minutes to make sure it dissolves. After 30 minutes, add the corn syrup; this will help prevent crystallization in the freezer. Gradually stir in the sugar until it is completely dissolved in the berry mixture.

Pour the jam into plastic or glass jars, leaving a ½-inch space at the top to allow for expansion in the freezer. Cover and let stand at room temperature for 24 hours or until jam has set. This jam will keep for 1 year in the freezer, or 3 weeks in the refrigerator.

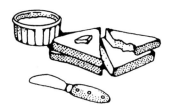

Index

A native of Orem, Utah, Jenny Stanger received a bachelor's degree in family life education from Brigham Young University. She also studied in Hawaii and China. Jenny has a passion for both family and food. For several years, she has taught culinary classes at Thanksgiving Point and other locations across Utah. Jenny also makes frequent Guest Chef appearances on ABC-4's *Good Things Utah*, KSL's *Studio 5*, and other television shows.

Jenny is passionate about strengthening the family. She also enjoys teaching Zumba, traveling, reading, and spending time outdoors. Jenny and her husband, Mark, reside in Elwood, Utah, with their four daughters.